LANGLEY & ROUND ABOUT

an illustrated community history of

Langley, Langley Green, Causeway Green & Rood End

Compiled & edited by
Suzie Drew & Diane Callow

in co-operation with
Langley Local History Society
in conjunction with Albright & Wilson

SANDWELL
Community
LIBRARIES

©1997

Sandwell Community Library Service ©1997

Published by:
Sandwell Community Library Service,
Library Support Services Section, Town Hall, High Street,
West Bromwich, West Midlands B70 8DX

ISBN: 1 900689 06 5

A C.I.P. record is available from the British Library

Printed in Langley by Anthony, Phillips & Davis,
23 Langley Green Road, Oldbury, West Midlands B69 4TG.

Editorial Committee chaired by Mr James Durrant; Terry Daniels, Suzie Drew, Eric W Fanthom, Bill Hipkiss, John Hodgkins, Pat Rodwell, John Sullivan, Audrey Taylor, Tom Tomlinson.

Langley Local History Society wish to acknowledge the commitment of Suzie Drew and Diane Callow in compiling this book and of Terry Daniels in compiling the index. Without their time and effort it would not have been possible.

We gratefully acknowledge the financial assistance from Albright & Wilson and a donation made in memory of the late Frank Noble, who was totally committed to the collection and preservation of local history material and would have heartily approved of this project.

I 0410862

Preface

Langley Local History Society began in 1996 when staff at Langley Library became aware of the true depth of local people's feelings about the area. The first meeting was held on St Valentine's Day 1996 and the small Reading Room bulged at the seams with more than thirty enthusiastic members. It was soon agreed that there was sufficient interest and commitment, not to mention material, to produce a booklet of local memories and a small Editorial Committee was formed. With the larger group meeting monthly and the smaller meeting weekly, the booklet "Langley & Langley Green Recalled" was printed in time for the Langley Christmas Lights celebrations at the end of November. Encouraged by being sold-out within two weeks, a second printing was rushed out before Christmas thanks to the efforts of the local printing firm.

The Editorial Committee, upset at how much good material had to be left out (due to lack of funding), determined to try for a second publication and Albright & Wilson kindly offered to fund printing costs. This new book was to be a "proper history of Langley, Langley Green, Causeway Green and Rood End" - little did we realise the extent of our undertaking! We have been forced to concede that a "proper history" of this area would require at the least a whole book each for these four much loved settlements. We have had to sadly admit that much still remains uncovered and unsaid, but hope that the reader will enjoy the memories and photographs included and perhaps be inspired to send us his or her own memories for inclusion in our Community History archive.

Suzie Drew, Community Librarian, Langley Library

Whilst the Editorial Committee has made every effort to verify the information given, the reader is asked to remember that many of the articles spring from memories of years gone by.

Contributors

Nancy Adams
Vera Angus
A V Baker
Laurence Banner
Curly Bastable
Derek Bastable
Miss G L Brant
John Bridge
Fred Broadbent
Hilda Broadbent
Elsie Cartwright
Derek Chambers
Peggy Cowley
Michael Cox
Jessie Crump
Jennifer Cullwick
Terry Daniels
Gwen Davis
Barbara Dunnett
Alex Durrant
James Durrant
Eric W Fanthom
Trevor Ford
Cyril Forrest
Peter Gaunt
Verna Gibbons
Florence Hadley
John Hadley
H G Hale
Bill Hipkiss
John Hodgkins
Bill Howen
Teresa Jaynes
Brian Jones
Mike Jones
Nancy Jones

Richard Landon
Naomi Lewis
Jean Line
Joyce Lloyd
Brenda McCrea
Robert Mellor
Sylvia Milner
Louisa Nash
Mera Newey
Ray Norris
Robert Oakes
Doris Pierce
Barbara Powell
Patricia Rickers
Pat Rodwell
Vera Round
Win Round
Brenda Salisbury
Margaret Shaw
Isabelle Shepherd
Bill Skett
Millie Smith
John Sullivan
Audrey Taylor
Tom Tomlinson
Emily Tranter
Wilfred Tranter
Jessie Warkup
Alan Watkins
Ray Watkins
George Webb
P West
Ann Whitlock
Barrie Willetts
Evelyn Wood
Zion United Reformed Church

Many other local people have contributed memories and information to our archives, but we regret that it has not been possible to include them in this book. This material may be seen at Langley Library and we hope to use it in future publications.

Contents

Sources of illustrations

Arthur Adams
N Adams
Audrey Allen
Dave Arnold
Jean Beckett
Barbara Beighton
Elsie Cartwright
Derek Chambers
Charles Cockbill
Peggy Cowley
K W Crump
Terry Daniels
Gwen Davis
Barbara Dunnett
Mrs Elliott
Eric W Fanthom
Florence Hadley
Bill Hipkiss
John Hodgkins

Teresa Jaynes
Nancy Jones
Naomi Lewis
Louisa Nash
Mera Newey
Doris Pierce
Barbara Powell
Pat Rodwell
Doreen Rogers
John Round
Win Round
Margaret Shaw
Isabelle Shepherd
Bill Skett
Judith Tranter
Jessie Warkup
Ray Watkins
R West

Albright & Wilson
Edward Street Methodist Church
Sandwell M B C
St Michael & All Angels
Warley Institutional Church
Zion United Reformed Church

Sandwell Civic Pictorial Record : p17 top, p20, p23, p35, p37, p50 top, p118, p140 top & bottom, p152, p174 top & bottom, p186 top & bottom, p188, p190, p191 top & bottom, p192 top & bottom.

These photographs represent a very small proportion of the photographs kindly loaned by members of the community. This is part of an ongoing project to preserve as many old photographs as possible. Copies can be seen at Langley Library. We hope to include more of these photographs in future publications.

Chapter One
Pre 1900

Langley: early beginnings

In the 8th or 9th century perhaps, somebody with a Saxon-sounding name, Wealuc, lived in this area, and since then the name in the form of Walloxhall, or Walloxhale, has been linked to Langley in historical narrative. The point of interest here is that such a person, being important enough to have his name bandied about in history, must have had an estate with a stretch of meadow land, with serfs, or villeins as they were called, and their dwellings. The suffix "hale" in Walloxhale refers to meadow land or hollow; most likely a long meadow, a "lang ley". I see that as the beginning of our village of Langley.

Langley is a common enough Anglo-Saxon place-name signifying a long pasture or clearing surrounded by woods or scrub land. Our Langley was first described as a manor in the 16th century, but before that it was regarded as the "green" part of Oldbury. In fact we can trace it back with some certainty to the early part of the Norman period when this particular Lang-Ley was part of the manor of Halas - Halesowen; and part of that parish until 1845. The Holy Trinity Church was consecrated in 1852. This new parish of Langley enveloped Rounds Green until 1905 when that itself became a parish, but in 1906 an area was gained from Quinton so that Moat Road came within our boundary, encompassing Barnford Hill, and up as far as Dog Kennel Lane.

The area was entirely rural in the early part of the 19th century, and well into this one there were quite a few farms about. In any case, there has always been the aura of a village about Langley, despite the accumulation of industry over the years, heavy, internationally renowned industry to boot. I expect it was then that Langley Green became just that in respect of Langley itself. In the dying years of the 20th century those works are gone, the buildings used for other purposes, or lie derelict, and only Albright & Wilson remains as a vibrant concern; so that the village atmosphere becomes more and more pronounced, thanks especially to efforts having been made recently towards that end.

Of the neighbouring areas, Causeway Green contains the most venerable place-name in the locality, Penncricket Lane. The name Penncrick, meaning the head or end of a boundary, being given by the British probably two thousand years ago, the "et" only making it easier to slip off the tongue.

Rood End is an interesting place that has had some factories within its bounds but not too much heavy industry, taking its name from the existence there at one time of a Holy Rood, or wayside cross. Whence, Crosswells in Langley, is an adjacent area to the cross.

The destiny of the district was sealed by the availability of the materials required for its prosperity, aided and abetted by the rail and canal systems. The air is cleaner now, the ambience more bright and pleasant - but for they who remember, no doubt the past has pride of place.

Let these pages rekindle flames for those for whom they once burned bright, and help others understand, and appreciate, the present.

Bill Hipkiss
based on F.W. Hackwood's "Oldbury and Round About"
and "A Parish Profile" by Rev. C.M. Beaver.

Rood End and the Last Rood

The Crosswell Spring at Langley is widely known of throughout the Langley and Oldbury area, but not too far away there once existed a stream of even greater fame, whose reputation is legendary - the stream of Rood End. Handed down tales tell of Crusaders travelling to Rood End to pray. The first Crusade began a thousand years ago in 1096, but even then Rood End settlement was about 400 years old, and it is from the name of this little hamlet that we can discover much information.

The "End" was the name Anglo-Saxons gave to their family settlements. Unlike the earlier Romans, they had no desire to build grand villas or crowded towns, instead they preferred to live in family groups. Anglo-Saxons began settling the Midlands area from about 600 AD. Their isolated villages are now absorbed into larger towns or cities, but the names still exist throughout the region. Thus we can deduce that people have inhabited Rood End for at least 1400 years.

The most important part of Rood End's name however is "Rood". Whether spelled Rood, Roode, Rude, Rode or Rod, this is the one and the same Anglo-Saxon word describing a wayside cross. The definition of a rood is a depiction of Jesus being crucified as a religious object - this being distinctly different from a plain cross with no figure. In rarer cases Christ was shown as a living being. In both instances though, Jesus would be painted as realistically as possible. Some of the statues were of carved wood, others made of cast metal, and above the head would be a little gable roof to protect the blessed work of art from weathering.

Most villages came to have their own cross at the market place, cross-roads or burial ground, but these once commonplace objects should not be confused with such high-status religious phenomenon as the roods. A rood was not raised due to a fashion, nor situated by mere chance; instead their sites proclaimed that something miraculous had occurred in the immediate area - such as a holy vision, or the curing of the sick.

Wayside roods became shrines in their own right as places for prayer and were often mentioned by pilgrims and priests as special places to which pilgrimages were made. There were two Holy Rood Days each year. Both of these days drew massive crowds where the rare roods existed and were accompanied by special Rood Fairs as part of the celebrations.

The Langley Rood was erected because a stream flowing there contained minerals which gave it medicinal properties. Anglo-Saxons always settled close to a clean water supply, and if that water was found to have healing qualities the source would be treated with high regard. As word spread the sick from further afield would visit to drink the water, seeking cures and relief from pain. The minerals contained in springs and streams tend to vary, so some would be beneficial for specific complaints - just as with the use of herbal remedies. This may seem rather far-fetched today due to advances made in medicine this century, but then it was a reality.

The Normans invaded Britain in 1066 and shared out the land amongst their nobles and high ranking soldiers - this included Oldbury of course. The First Crusade began in 1096 and the Eighth (and final) Crusade in 1270. Old folk tales usually have some basis of truth, and if those concerning Rood End and the Crusaders are founded upon fact, then the Normans had also come to regard that special stream as sacred. All Crusaders were required to perform a ritual

4

cleansing of their bodies before departing, but this was not simply a quick scrub in the nearest duck pond. The water used had to be "holy" and therefore pure to symbolise their holy intentions.

The reason the Rood of Rood End no longer exists stems back to 1534, when Henry Vlll of England split from the Roman Catholic Church, because the Pope would not approve his application for a divorce. He carried out the Reformation, setting up the Church of England and put himself in charge. Ancient monasteries were demolished. Surviving churches were drastically altered; Oldbury Chapel was not built until 1529, in 1547 workmen were plied with drink then sent to destroy all "Popish" (i.e. Catholic) figures and plaster over the beautiful murals. (This chapel was on the site of the old Public Buildings next to Savacentre).

The Rood itself might have survived another forty years though, as in 1587 there came the order "All Roodes, all images of Saintes should be defaced". It was at this time that most village crosses not standing on consecrated ground were pulled down, because they too depicted carvings of figures, not just a full statue. The crosses were replaced with cones, pinnacles, spheres or even signposts for travellers. Hence, most village crosses seen today are not actually crosses as such.

The original nucleus of Rood End seems to have been centred around the present day Vernon Road and the Gate Inn - just where both parts of Rood End converge; and both that part running from St Paul's Road and that which begins at Tat Bank Road are ancient thoroughfares. As they meet at the vicinity of the original hamlet the rood would have stood nearby.

The King's map maker during 1675 was John Ogilby, and one of his maps was the road from London to Shrewsbury. Ogilby only included well known landmarks and their distances along the route, so travellers knew how far they still had to travel. Although the rood itself was long gone the minute village of Rood End appears on the map.

Local people would have continued to use the stream of pure water for domestic purposes and, although there were no religious connections by 1675, people would have regarded certain waters as good for the health and digestion. The horses pulling stage coaches needed regular rests and watering; and travellers who made regular journeys appreciated clean drinking water - some would still be visiting Rood End especially to "take the waters".

The rights of ordinary people to have unpolluted water to drink in Langley were never written down - and they were duped by the promises made by the new breweries that their domestic supplies would continue. Breweries need a plentiful supply of good water to produce good beer. On the 1857 map of Oldbury and Langley a stream runs along Rood End Road towards the Bell Inn; curiously it vanishes just behind the pub. The waters of the Crosswell were similarly taken for brewing in 1857. The Bell Inn itself was probably built in 1840.

The reduction of water had a knock-on effect - water sellers did a roaring trade with water hauled from Rounds Green and poor folk often died of dysentery, gastro-enteritis and even cholera. There was no mains water supply laid on in the Oldbury and Langley area until the start of the present century,

The next time you pass along Dudley Road into Birmingham have a glance at the rood that stands outside St Patrick's Roman Catholic Church and when you next see the

Bell Inn or the Gate at Rood End think of our lost treasures; the Rood and the stream are no more.

Verna Gibbons

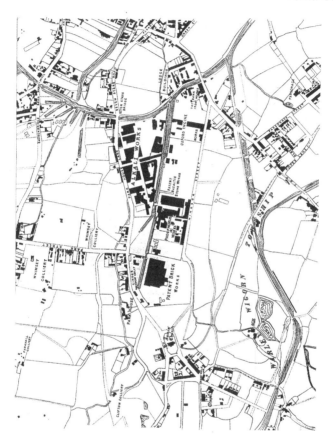

Map of Langley of 1857 showing Langley Pool and the Mill. Windsor St. later became Trinity St. The church named as St. James is actually Holy Trinity. The original Albright & Wilson site, formerly part of the Park House estate, was bought from Chance Brothers c. 1853.

The story of the Zion Church, Langley Green - the first church in Langley and life at the time

About 1775 a Moravian Minister preached the gospel under a large tree on "The Green". It could have been a mature oak, which would have provided shelter in bad weather. Could this perhaps have stood where the present Royal Oak pub stands today? (It is recorded that the tree was blown down on 5th November 1800). At this time there was no other church in Langley. The nearest was an Anglican - the Chapel of Ease, which stood near the present Savacentre in Oldbury.

In those days Langley Green was just a small village in the midst of farmlands. The only road of note was a secondary one from Halesowen to Oldbury via Blackheath. Plans of the old cottages, which stood alongside the betting shop until 1967, show a pedestrian right of way along Chapel Passage from a very narrow Langley Green Road. This was part of a footway to Halesowen.

The Old Mill, ca 1777-1785

Mill Lane once housed quite a few families and is surely the site of the Old Water Mill to which the Langley Green fellowship turned to hold their services of worship about 1777. The pool was situated alongside the canal, at the rear of Albright & Wilson's car park. The area abounds with "watery" names: Moat Farm, Moat Road, Reservoir Road, Barnford Park, Titford Road etc. Titford Pool was the natural watershed.

The people would be mostly unschooled, both men and women probably working 6 or 7 day weeks. They had no musical instruments and probably only a couple of Bibles between them. Those who could read would have to do the leading. They would know little of events further afield, such as the American War of Independence.

The Barn at Smethwick, ca1786-1790

For some reason (perhaps rental costs or lack of space), they had to seek a new meeting place. They faced a walk of nearly 2 miles to a barn near the Old Church at Smethwick in the Church Road/Uplands area. Here they installed rough benches and a make-shift pulpit.

In those days the Smethwick area was little populated, the 1801 census shows 1,100 inhabitants, Oldbury had even less. Factory-type employment was in its infancy at Boulton's Soho Foundry. Both towns grew dramatically over the next 30 years. The Barn stood in the shadow of the local Anglican church. Records state that a man called Stanley was determined to drive away these "Methodists" and eventually had his way.

The Cottage at the Dogkennel, ca 1790-1791

The fellowship, led by Rev. John Hammond, found a cottage at the Dogkennel (surely Dogkennel Lane) and were able to meet for worship morning and afternoon on Sundays. The Dogkennel in those days was the kennels for the local hunt and located on the site of the present Merrivale Inn. The accommodation was probably cramped but had two merits, it was less walking and it was also well away from the "Established Church" buildings. This was a time when the Lord's Day was little celebrated by the general populace. The coarse pursuits of many of the people of that day would offend practising Christians, who would often be the subject of scorn and derision.

The Thatched Cottage, Langley Green Road, ca 1792-1798

The fellowship moved again, this time to a thatched cottage in Langley Green Road. James Cotterell, a working man, became minister, a post which he continued for over forty years.

The last quarter of the 18th century saw the appalling treatment of workers during the early years of the Industrial Revolution. The newly mechanised mills of Lancashire and Yorkshire, the slave trade out of Liverpool and the creation of the Black Country around the Staffordshire coal and iron fields, Northern Worcestershire and North Warwickshire with its great industrial capital, Birmingham.

Langley Green was not to be influenced by the physical changes taking place for some years yet, being somewhat out on a limb. Under the leadership of James Cotterell, the fellowship soon prospered numerically and financially enough to plan a permanent but small meeting place.

The First Chapel: Zion Independent Chapel, ca 1798-1827

A small piece of land 8 yards by 8 yards on the south-west side of the footway leading into Causeway Green Road was leased. The lease was signed on 21st November 1796 by James Cotterell and James Samuel Hanson, Trustees. Landlords were Martha, Mark and John Postons, "In consideration of £3 4s 0d of good and lawful money of Great Britain, and the sum of Two Pence every 29th day of September each year." The chapel, built by Thomas Jackson (one of the founders), was opened on 29th October 1798.

At this time the Stourbridge Railway (later GWR) had not been cut. Langley Green Road was then on a level with Uncle Ben's Bridge. Moat Road was a narrow lane with high hedges. Within easy access of the chapel area and village green were rural scenes. The majority were poor working people. Every house had its baking oven.

This small chapel (accommodating 150 persons) was afterwards enlarged, but with continued growth of the fellowship a new building had to be considered.

In 1805 the Sunday School began. A small building had been erected for this purpose and there were only 16 children. The teachers, who walked from Birmingham every Sunday morning, were paid a small sum for their services and used to go to the Old Cross Inn for lunch. The school building was enlarged in 1828.

The Second Chapel
The first building was replaced in 1828 at a cost of £198 9s 3d. James Cotterell continued his ministry until his death in 1833. Twelve years later, on 3rd August 1845, Rev. Clement Pass came to Langley Green. There was poverty in Langley Green and Mr Pass had a sum of money given to him by one of the firms in the locality for weekly distribution to the poor. Not everyone could read and write and the help and advice of the minister was of great benefit.

In 1837 the Titford canal was opened. The canal constructors had arranged a "feeder line" via the six locks in the Birmingham/Wolverhampton canal. The top lock is 511ft. above sea level. An early steam pumping engine made at Boulton & Watt's Foundry (Soho) was used to pump the water back up the locks. The Titford project brought in "navvies" for work on the cut and later the construction of the Stourbridge railway, which was later to revolutionise the area.

The Jubilee of the school was celebrated on the first Sunday in June 1855, when special services were held. The children marched in procession through the village, headed by a new banner. Each child wore a medal, which had been specially struck to commemorate the Jubilee. A larger school building was erected in 1860.

The last services in the old chapel were held on 1st April 1877.

The Third Chapel

A larger, more extensive chapel was planned, foundation stones were laid on 11th June 1877 and the chapel was opened on 2nd June 1878.

The Third Chapel (built 1877) & adjoining schoolrooms to the left (built 1860)

The Rev. Clement Pass died in 1889 and in 1890 the Deacons agreed to engage a retired Baptist minister, Rev. David

Jeavons, for 6 months at 10/- per week. This arrangement continued for 17 years!

Holy Trinity, Langley : A Pretty Little Village Church

If you stand outside the "Model" public house (formerly the "Queen's Head") at Langley and gaze towards Trinity Street, there is a traffic island that lies between - this was the Holy Trinity Church and its burial ground.

So many people were moving into the area in the 1840s that it was necessary to build a church for Langley. Although an application to build was granted on 23rd December 1845 and Lord Lyttleton laid the first stone that same year, it took seven years to raise the money to complete the construction work due to the extravagant costs. The price of stone was rising continuously and most new churches were being built of brick with stonework dressings only on windows, doorways or corners - as with St. Michael's (Langley) and Christ Church (Oldbury).

No expense was to be spared for Holy Trinity, and it was destined to be one of the last stone churches built. Had the site not been donated by the owner of the nearby Park House, they would have been even higher: compare the building costs :-

Church	When opened	Number of seats	Building costs
Christ Church (Oldbury)	1841	1400	£4500
Holy Trinity (Langley)	1852	500	£6000
St. Michael (Langley)	1890	700	£5500

13

Had Holy Trinity had a tower (as have the other two) the price would have been closer to £10,000. Its lack of a tower gave the illusion of an even smaller building; instead it had a quaint little bell-gable over its western end, which made the porch on the sunny south side a prominent feature of the church, which was built of a beautiful white stone.

Bishop Pepys of Worcester consecrated the church and burial ground in 1852. There was an income of £160 a year to pay for a vicar. This had risen to £170 by 1874. In 1860 the grounds were planted with 12 poplar trees, the cost was 6 shillings.

The grounds of the church measured just over half an acre. It was turned into an "island" when Park (House) Lane was re-aligned and Trinity Street (formerly Windsor Street) was completed. In that tiny patch which surrounded Holy Trinity are buried 871 people. The final interment in 1898 was that of the first vicar, Rev. William Laing, who was laid to rest with other members of his family.

Of the 871 buried there, 817 were children below the age of 16, 434 of whom did not survive until their first birthday.

When St. Michael's was opened in 1891 it was appointed the new Parish Church of Langley; Holy Trinity was accordingly demoted to be a chapel of ease to St. Michael's.

Verna Gibbons

Holy Trinity Church, Langley, showing the bell-gable & porch

Holy Trinity Church, Langley interior (before the organ was installed)

Living conditions of the time

In 1855 a large number of the principal ratepayers and magistrates petitioned the General Board of Health to investigate the local sanitary conditions, in view of the alarming rate of mortality.

The report of the Inspector who conducted an enquiry on 7th November 1855, reveals that there were no public lights, no scavenging or refuse removal, no system of sewerage or sewers; the roads had no gutters and no paved footpaths, and were the receptacles for every kind of filth injurious to health; many cellars were full of stagnant water, and there was an absence of proper privies.

Although a private company obtained powers under an Act of 1853, they did not supply water, and the inhabitants derived their only supply from "Rounds Green Springs" at the rate of one shilling per hundred gallons from water carriers.

taken from the Charter Souvenir 1935

Bethel Chapel, Langley

Membership of this church began in 1850, when worshippers met in a private house in Whyley Street. A few years later the members built a chapel in the same street using funds raised by doing extra "skip" work at various local collieries - thus it was known for some time as the "Skip Chapel".

In 1877 this Methodist New Connexion Church obtained a new site on the corner of Broad Street and Arden Grove and a chapel was built at the cost of about £1700. An organ was installed at the cost of about £300, "which for some time was considered the best in the district". The old chapel in Whyley Street was enlarged and extended for use as a schoolroom. The chapel had borrowed £1000 on mortgage, but in 1897 the friends of the church, by spreading their contributions over three years, managed to raise £600. As the result of a public appeal and of contributions by Albright & Wilson, Chance & Hunt, Showells Brewery and Edwin Danks by 1900 the chapel was free from debt.

taken from "Picturesque Oldbury" by Henry McKean

Bethel Chapel, Whyley Street (later the Sunday School) built 1855

Bethel Chapel, Broad Street - now a warehouse

The Zion Chapel, Rood End

John Wesley paid several visits to the Black Country between 1738 and 1790, and the first Methodist Chapel was in fact built in the region at Tipton in 1755. The movement spread rapidly and was very firmly established by the end of the eighteenth century. Some dissent was however apparent because of the absolute power held by the hierarchy of the movement. "Break away" groups were formed, amongst them The New Connexion Methodists, the Primitive Methodists, and later the Wesleyan Reform Union.

The Wesleyan Reform Union had its roots in the industrial region of Yorkshire, the eleventh such Union was founded in a miner's cottage in Collier's Row, Albert Street, Oldbury on the 7th May 1865. The members moved to Canal Street, and then to rooms above the "Why-Not-Inn" public house in Talbot Street, and finally a chapel was built in Hunt Street, which was opened on 14th February 1875. Membership grew very quickly, more room was needed, and so it was decided in 1880 to start a new meeting place away from the Hunt Street Chapel. Members houses were used in the Rood End area, and then a permanent room was acquired above a shop in Vicarage Road. Joseph Massey, a Union stalwart for many years recalled preaching his first sermon "for the cause" in this room in 1887.

A permanent place of worship was of course a priority. The "Weekly News" of 13th September 1890 reported that "... the foundation stone of a new mission in connection with the Wesley Reformers was laid on Monday 8th September in Vicarage Road, Rood End by Mr G Wheeler of Birmingham." The Rev. Whitehouse reported to those present that £250 had been raised and that all the bricks, lime, sand and fittings had been donated by local businessmen, and that "gentlemen" had given labouring money. A tea and public meeting was held in an adjoining field where the sum of £9 7s 1d was raised.

The original conveyance of the land was strict in that "... religion according to the late John Wesley only, was to be practised on the land". Building proceeded very quickly and the new Zion Chapel was opened on Sunday 7th December 1890. The building itself was very simple in design, and was to be used in pursuance of religion according to Wesley for many years.

The original trustees were a diverse body drawn from the local community, with professions such as glassmaker, engineer, moulder, nail-maker, cooper, bootmaker, farm labourer, blacksmith and "dissenting Minister".

from a short history of the Zion, Rood End by the late Miss Jessie Crump (by kind permission of her brother).

Causeway Green Methodist Chapel

Before 1863 the nearest Methodist Chapel to Causeway Green was in George Road, Warley. Every Sunday Methodists from the village made their way up Pound Road, then a country lane, past the "Plough" Inn and then up George Road to the top of the hill. There were no street lights or public transport and in wintertime the journey was difficult and unpleasant, particularly for the elderly. It was soon realised that the village needed a chapel of its own. Worshippers began to meet every Sunday in the cottage of Mr H Parkes in Ashes Road. The cottage has long since been demolished to widen the railway bridge. After a time they purchased the land on which the chapel now stands but the car park area was not purchased until 15 years later.

Mr Henry Parkes was so anxious to see the church built that he put in the foundations himself - without official permission. However he was a builder and they were allowed to stay and, after begging most of the materials, he supervised the building of the chapel - his workmen all giving a day's labour free. The original chapel was very small and the second side-window from the door marks the limit of the first phase of the building. The original cost of the chapel was £170.

It was opened for worship on 18th October 1863. The preachers were the Rev. H Fish and the Rev. J S Ridsdale. The total collections for the day amounted to £27 7s 11d, a marvellous sum in those days.

Causeway Green Chapel before restoration in 1963

The work prospered and membership increased and between 1891 and 1893 the building was enlarged. The cost was £164 17s 0d All accounts were settled before the renovation was complete. Candles were used for lighting until 1876 when oil lamps were installed. In 1903 a gas main was laid in the lane and the chapel was then lit by gas lamps. Coal and coke stoves were used to heat the church.

John Hadley

Spring Street Methodist, Langley

The Primitive Methodists from Green Street in Oldbury introduced their cause into Langley in the early 1850s. Services were held in a house in High Street, Langley until a "school-chapel" was erected in Spring Street in 1861.

In 1872 a new chapel was built by Mr John Sadler. (The same building has been renovated to form the Barlow Playhouse today).

from "Picturesque Oldbury" by Henry McKean

Edward Street Methodist Church, Langley

Worship began in 1885 in a house in Henry Street, now demolished. Numbers grew so that larger premises were needed. Use of the upper floor of a carpenter's workshop at the top of Edward Street was obtained by Samuel Whitehouse, who also owned land on which the present church was built at the cost of some £600 in 1896.

from the Edward Street Church Centenary Display

St Michael & All Angels, Langley

St Michael's was built in 1889-90 on a field known as "Green Robins" or "Clover Piece" adjacent to new housing.

According to Alexander M Chance, chairman of the Committee in the appeal leaflet:- "The new church for Langley Green is situated in the Black Country, in the parish of Langley, and in the County and Diocese of Worcester.

"Langley was taken from the mother parish of Halesowen and made into a separate district in 1845. For four-and-a-half years a licensed room was used for services, and in 1852 the present parish church (*Holy Trinity*) was consecrated, and the district of Langley converted into an ecclesiastical parish, the endowment being provided from the funds of the Ecclesiastical Commissioners.

"The population of Langley being at that time comparatively small, a church was built capable of holding about 500 persons, but the rapid growth of the parish, the population now being estimated at 10,000, has made additional church accommodation a matter of absolute necessity.

"The new church (*St. Michael's*) will eventually become the mother church of the parish, and the present church will be used as a Chapel of Ease."

The main industries of the area were chemical works, brick yards, glass works, breweries, iron works, engineering works and collieries. The site was given by Mrs Mary Barrs, in a rapidly growing part of the parish and in close proximity to Langley Green, Causeway Green and Bristnall Fields. She also gave sufficient adjoining land to build schools and a parish room, when funds could be obtained.

The first vicar of Langley was William Laing, who was vicar of Holy Trinity Church from 1846 until he retired in 1888. He was the last person to be buried in Holy Trinity churchyard in1898. Michael Pryor was the second vicar of Langley and the first of St Michael's from 1888 until 1902.

taken from "St. Michael & All Angels' Langley: a parish profile" by Rev. C.M. Beaver

St. Michael & All Angels' Church & Schools

St. Michael's Mixed Schools, Langley

These were built in 1893 to accommodate 300 children. In 1896 the Infant School was added with accommodation for 200. In 1899 the schools were again enlarged, with accommodation for a further 100.

Holy Trinity Schools, Langley

These schools for mixed and infants were erected in 1899 to accommodate 336 children and were situated opposite Holy Trinity Church in Titford Road. During the Great War they were occupied by Belgian refugees and became known locally as the "Belgian Schools". Later they were used for catering by the school meals service and during the depression as a social and training centre for people out of work.

British School, Langley

This school was erected by the Primitive Methodists in 1872 on a site in Spring Street purchased in 1870 at the cost of £170. The main building cost £700. In 1874 the Chance Brothers rented the premises and opened them as an infants' school, but they were closed again in 1879. The trustees applied successfully to the Education Department to come on the annual grant list and duly appointed Mr Poynton as their first headmaster. The school was opened as a mixed department with the fees ranging from 2d to 6d per week. In 1880 a small classroom was built and in 1886 the infants' department was erected at a cost of £300. The boundary of the playground was made up of old railway sleepers until Langley Park was opened in 1886 , when they were replaced by a fence or iron railings.

all three articles taken from "Picturesque Oldbury" by Henry McKean

Langley Railways

At the beginning of 1866 the Stourbridge Railway Company had constructed and opened its line from a junction with the Great Western Railway (GWR) at Stourbridge to Old Hill.

The railway arrived at Langley as a result of the Stourbridge Company being authorised to extend its line from

Old Hill to Galton Junction at West Smethwick, connecting with the London and North Western Railway (LNWR) main line from Birmingham to Wolverhampton. The course of the line was the same as it is now.

Langley was served quite well by the new railway, having two stations - one called "Oldbury & Langley Green" and one called "Rood End". Rood End station was where Rood End Road crosses the railway by the Pel Company office block.

The line was opened on 1st April 1867. On the same day the LNWR introduced a through train service from New Street, Birmingham via Langley to Stourbridge and beyond to Hereford, with 7 trains each way on weekdays and 4 each way on Sundays.

The new railway was not entirely without critics. The Dudley Herald reported that at the first meeting of the Oldbury Local Board of Health on 5th April 1867:

"The Clerk reported writing to and calling upon 'the Board of Trade with reference to the neglect of the Stourbridge Railway Co. to provide bridges, adding that from information he had received it appeared they had no power to compel them to do so. If bridges were necessary it should have been provided that they be erected at the time the companies bill was passed."

This must be referring to Langley, as it was the only part of Oldbury through which the railway passed.

At the same meeting concerning business connected with canals it was stated that:

"The canal companies along with the railway companies will do nothing unless they are obliged".

In October 1824 all canal companies were urged to oppose any railway development proposal. The Titford Canal

Project tell us in their booklet "The Titford Project" that the Titford valley was surveyed for the canal, partly to prevent encroachment into the area by the Birmingham, Wolverhampton and Dudley Railway, and that the survey was carried out at the end of 1846.

The Stourbridge Railway coming to Langley and Smethwick was just what the canal company was trying to prevent. In 1870 the Stourbridge Railway Company was absorbed by the GWR and took its place in history.

Three years later the surprisingly named "Dudley & Oldbury Junction Railway " company, obtained permission to construct a branch line from a junction with the GWR at Langley Green to Oldbury. In 1876 an agreement was reached with the GWR to operate the line when opened. The branch line company title was changed to the Oldbury Railway in 1881.

A further three years later "Oldbury & Langley Green" station was renamed "Langley Green" and the branch line was opened for goods train services.

Langley Green Station was originally adjacent to the level crossing at Station Road and in May 1885 the station site was moved about 220 yards eastwards and built as a junction station with the Oldbury branch line. By that month the line from Langley into Oldbury was fully operational for goods and passenger train services. On 1st May Rood End Station was closed.

The Oldbury branch railway was an independent concern for about forty years, which was longer than most by a long way, and was finally absorbed by the GWR in the summer of 1894. The services continued to operate on the Oldbury branch until March 1915, when the passenger service was discontinued. As many people will remember, goods trains continued working to the goods yard at Inkerman Street, Oldbury until well after the Second World War.

There was another branch line into Oldbury from Langley. From the bridge carrying Rood End Road over the railway looking west, there is a crank in the fence around the BIP works. It is obvious that a railway line once went into the works. It did, and continued to cross Pope's Lane and Parsonage Street and served the Midland Tar Distillers Plant between Birmingham Road and the long gone Tat Bank Village. This branch was, of course, purely industrial.

Looking towards Birmingham from the same bridge there is a distinct cut-away part of the embankment on the Stourbridge-bound lineside, with a few decaying remains of wooden fencing. That must almost certainly be the site of the down-line Rood End Station platform. On the other side of the railway can be seen a small factory railway loading bay and a run of track sunk in the floor. The siding trucks used to be shunted there by a road or farm type tractor.

At the level crossing in Station Road, it is also still possible to see the impression of the Stourbridge-bound platform of the original "Oldbury & Langley Green" Station on the bank between the railway and the footpath to Avery Dennison Works (formerly Myers, and now a new housing development), which originally went up to the platform of the present station with access to Myers. The blue brick building used by the metals handling concern by the level crossing was the stables of the railway company horses.

Ray Norris

Langley Green Station Names

1st April 1867 - when the line opened, it was named "Oldbury & Langley Green".

7th November 1884 - renamed "Langley Green".

January 1904 - renamed "Langley Green & Rood End".

6th January 1936 - reverted to "Oldbury & Langley Green".

Langley Green & Rood End Station - Mark Tatton (on the right) was the stationmaster and retired in 1924 after 40 years service at Langley Green. He was a member of the Royal Antediluvian Order of Buffaloes and president of the Rood End Permanent Money Society.

The "Big Stack" at Albright & Wilson - Oldbury Works

The "Big Albright Stack" our 251 foot chimney, was erected in 1872 by the Langley building contractors, Jackson Bros. It became a famous landmark both in the local community and as far afield as the Clent Hills.

It was designed by W J Macquorn Rankine, the well known Glasgow civil engineer. His hand written specification for the structure covers eight pages and details every aspect of the construction, for example *"The Bricks - of regular feature with plane surfaces, straight edges, and sharp, square corners; free from flaws and giving a clear ringing sound when struck"*.

The actual process of bricklaying for the great chimney was set out by W J Macquorn Rankine in considerable detail. Excavation, iron hooping, scaffolding, even the lightening conductor were clearly specified in his very clear hand.

"At no time shall the building be carried on at a more rapid rate than six feet of vertical height per day".

We can estimate that the work took about three months to complete. The original specification was dated 26th July 1872 and the whole structure completed before the end of the year. At 251 feet the stack was, in its time, the second tallest in the country. (The Stoke Prior chimney at Droitwich was a few feet taller). It contained half a million bricks and was built in two sections up to a height of 80 feet.

The whole structure cost £1,586 payable one month after completion!

The stack was designed to give a good draught to four phosphorus furnace fires radiating for considerable distances from its base. Until superseded in the 1890s by a continuous electrothermic process, distillation of phosphorus from banks of clay retorts was the only method of manufacture. The original raw material was bone ash.

Examples of the clay retorts still exist, one at least in pristine condition. They were bottle shaped - some 48 inches long by 8 inches internal diameter - and made from a special fireclay material. (The making of these retorts was, in itself, an art. The clay took many months of preparation and construction involved the careful treading of the base by expert pot-makers. The retorts were made on site and burnt to biscuit condition in beehive kilns each holding about 100 retorts).

The retorts were filled with a black powder, produced by drying a mixture of concentrated phosphoric acid and ground coal, charcoal or other carbon. They were then built into galley-type direct fired coal furnaces. Each furnace held twenty four of them.

Under the intense heat from the coal fire below, drawn by the mighty 251 feet stack above, the phosphorus vapour was produced. It was ducted through short cast-iron necks which in turn connected with water cooled condensers running the full length of each furnace. The phosphorus collecting in the bottom of the condensers was ladled out into cast-iron bowls by "ladling cans".

In the early days the main use of phosphorus was in match making. Very soon however the element was used in manufacture of a very wide range of very useful products in industry and in the home.

Tom Tomlinson

30

Changing Phosphorus Retorts in 1890 - George Harris & Co.

This fine looking team of workmen, armed with tongs and tampers, was led by foreman George Ankers.

Flat caps and mufflers were the order of the day. Heavy tweed trousers were worn as a protection against any flying sparks. Those same Harris Tweed trousers were still worn by men handling phosphorus until the 1980s.

Each furnace was changed three times a week, changing days being Monday, Wednesday and Friday mornings. Working on the phosphorus furnaces was very skilled. Once the phosphorus had been produced it had to be purified, handled, stored and despatched under water.

George Ankers, George Harris and the rest of the retort changing team, knew their job, respected phosphorus and worked safely.

Tom Tomlinson

Billy James - Albright & Wilson Boy Gate-Keeper 1896

This photograph was one from several albums of photographs of Albright & Wilson staff and work people, which were formally presented to William Arthur Albright, and which he particularly prized.

Standing on a heap of coal in front of a wall decorated with a poster probably advertising a Worker's Outing, Billy looks confident and self assured. His sign of office is proudly displayed.

The works hours were 6.00am to 5.00 p.m. and Billy would open and close the gate at exactly those times. The Works Bell hung in a belfry over the entrance to the Works Stores. The Bell was later replaced by a steam whistle to mark the start and end of each work day.

Work people, arriving after the bell had rung were not allowed into the Works. Deprived of a day's work, they described themselves as "bell-cast".

Tom. Tomlinson

Frederick Kinchin - Foreman at Albright & Wilson

Frederick Kinchin, my paternal great, great grandfather was born at Northfield in 1830 and when he married Mary Ann Birch in Birmingham in 1853, he was already a chemical worker.

His childhood was spent in Selly Oak, where in 1844 Arthur Albright persuaded his partners John and Edmund Sturge to undertake the making of phosphorus. During 1854 Arthur Albright severed his connections with John and Edmund Sturge. On the dissolution of their partnership Sturge retained the name and their traditional manufactures and Arthur Albright took the Selly Oak Works and soon transferred it to Langley.

Frederick and Mary Ann Kinchin had eleven children. Census returns show them living in the "Crosswells" Inn, Hobicus Lane, Langley in 1861 with their four young sons and a young servant. His profession is described as "victualler". In the 1870s they were living in Park Lane, Langley and by 1881 they were sharing the Mill House, Hobicus Lane with Henry Hough, a chemical worker and James Russell, a brewers drayman. By this time Frederick Kinchin was a manufactures foreman at Albright & Wilson, where his sons Alfred and Thomas also worked. The partner's salaries book mentions a Fred Kinchin, who as foreman earned from £104 to £156 per annum.

Frederick Kinchin died at 47 Vicarage Road on 4th December 1901 aged 72 years.

Jean Mary Line (née Kinchin)

British Industrial Plastics - small beginnings

"It was just a small piece of land - a narrow strip of waste land bounded on two sides by a canal which turned at right-angles and at the far end by the wall of the phosphorus works of Albright & Wilson Ltd. Along the fourth side was the Great Western Railway Company's line between Langley Green and Oldbury, on which ran, to and fro, a one-coach motor train, known in the local dialect as the "Owdbury Dodger".

"Unimportant though the site seemed in the year 1894 ... here was erected the small privately owned factory which, in the fullness of time and after many ups and downs, was to develop into the great BIP Group.

"Situated in Tat Bank Road, Oldbury, the site was somewhat unique in that one had to cross a drawbridge over the canal to reach it.

"On the opposite side of the canal were the lead chambers of the sulphuric acid plant of Chance and Hunt Ltd.

"In those early days when the word 'Plastics' bore but slight, if any, significance in the industrial world, BIP was known as "The British Cyanides Company Limited". Little then did any one dream of the lines along which the company would finally develop.

"But first the reason why the Company was formed at all should be recorded. In about 1890 the gold-mining countries, notably South Africa, adopted a process involving the use of cyanide for the extraction of gold from low-grade ores. This opened up possibilities for chemical manufacturers and the two neighbouring Oldbury firms, Chance and Hunt Ltd. and Albright and Wilson Ltd., both started experimenting in the production of cyanide. These two neighbours decided to pool their efforts in this direction by jointly forming a small separate company which they named "The British Cyanides Company Limited". Plant was installed on the narrow piece of land appropriately adjacent to the works of both parent firms".

taken from "The Story of B.I.P." by Cyril S. Dingley

Work on the farm

Farms abounded in the area and there was seasonal work to be had at times.

Dumb Sal's Farm in Causeway Green Road, between Hadley Street and the "Hen & Chickens" public house. Otherwise known as "Blindfold Farm". Sal was Jack Hadley's deaf housekeeper.

My great-grandmother Louisa Oliver came to Langley from Oakham in Rutland when she was quite young. My father told me that she walked all the way. She worked in the fields at Whitehouse's farm and lost the sight in one eye in an accident.

Barbara Powell

Louisa Oliver at work on Whitehouse's farm ...

... and in her Sunday best

36

Farm workers at Leahouse Farm, Pound Road at the turn of the century.

Official opening of Langley Park 4th August 1886

In the edition of 7th August 1886 The Weekly News carried an extensive article on "the public opening of the handsome, though small park which has been prepared and laid out by Mr Arthur Albright, for the use of the people of Langley for ever.

"There was not a street, and scarcely a house in Langley where the people did not express their thankfulness and appreciation for what has been done for them by suspending a flag or motto through their window, or across the street where they reside. The bunting therefore was all that could be desired, and at intervals were found such mottoes as - 'Blessed is he that considereth the poor' (and) "Arthur Albright forever'...

"In place of the objectionable ditch, which ran through the ground, and was a constant danger to the health of the people in the vicinity, a large drain has been laid down, carrying the water in fair weather into the small pool, which is one of the chief features of ornamentation.".. Mr Albright by his generosity has not only provided for the health and pleasure of the people of Langley for all time to come, but by insisting on the whole of the work being done by those out of regular employment, has very considerably relieved the prevailing distress of the district.

"The Canal Company very generously gave up about a quarter of an acre of land on their side of the park to allow the boundary to be straightened and enlarged, and the whole has been fenced in with ornamental iron railings, all along High Street with stone base set upon bricks, all firmly and substantially erected".

The dignitaries at the opening ceremony are all listed and include such notable names as Arthur Albright, W.A. Albright, G. Stacey Albright, J.E. Wilson, J.W. Wilson, Frederick Chance, Edward Chance and Walter Showell.

The speeches are all reported. "Mr Arthur Albright wished to say ... that they fully recognised their duties to their workpeople, and it was chiefly for them that this ground had been given. There were a large number of their workpeople around that place, so that there must be some thousands of their children which he hoped would be sent to play there instead of in the streets. It would be kind to the newly-laid turf, however, if it were left to itself for a short time until its fibres got well set ...

"The Rev. W Laing said he had been in the parish just 42 years, and he thanked God that he had put it into the heart of Mr Albright to give them such a beautiful place. They were all fond of natural scenery, and he hoped that many of the people would be led to raise their aspirations higher than before. He did not want to be a rebel in the camp, but he would suggest that the name of Mr Albright should be connected with that place. 12 years ago there were 9,000 people in the parish of Oldbury, but now there were more than 20,000. In those days it was a natural thing to see the colliers going about on Sunday with their dogs and cocks, which they trained to fight, and the men also fought together as a common occurrence. A friend told him that at one time they could walk through Langley on the Sunday without the slightest indication that it was the Lord's day. In those days there was house after house with no Bible to be found in it, and even if there were, very few could read it. He remembered some people at Oldbury thinking that they could change all this in a short time, and do everything, but they found their mistake, and the improvement was a gradual one. He sincerely hoped that their future would be a happy one, that God would bless the giver of that place, and that ministers and people would do their duty better in the future".

After the speeches "... the party strolled round the grounds and came to the entrance in High Street, when the Crosswells Brewery's excellent band, augmented by members of the Village Band, marched up, and the gates were thrown open to the public, who had been anxiously waiting on the outside. The band, under the leadership of Mr Jewkes, took up its position on an elevated piece of land, and played some fine selections of music in the course of the evening".

The Weekly News 4th August 1886

Langley Band

A very early photograph of the Langley Prize Band, which was founded in 1878

Inns & Taverns:
"The Last Inn"

"The Last Inn" in Mill Lane in the late 1800s.

This building stood on the corner of Mill Lane and Station Road. The site was later occupied by the Hughes Johnson offices. The landlady's son (above centre) was over six feet tall and was known locally as the "Gentle Giant". The name Daniel Felkin is just distinguishable on the Inn sign.

Isabelle Shepherd

The Fountain Inn

Regulars at the Fountain Inn in Pit Lane, later renamed High Street.
The Fountain Inn was reputedly built in the mid 1800s by Joe Jackson, who was landlord for over 20 years and had quite a reputation for his home brewed ales.

The photograph shows Mr William Swancott (seated to far right), who was landlord later and Sid Lewis (2nd row, 4th from right), his son-in-law. The building was later transformed into the Langley Post Office.

Isabelle Shepherd

Sid Lewis, probably at the back of the Fountain Inn in the late 1890s

Sid Lewis came to the Midlands from Wales to look for work at the age of 16 in about 1893. He lodged at the Fountain Inn, where he met, and in 1903 married, the landlord's daughter Isabella Swancott. He was a very keen gardener and often won prizes for his vegetables. He also worked at Albright & Wilson for a long time as a plumber.

Isabelle Shepherd

The Railway Tavern
The Railway Tavern pub stood quite close to the Zion Church in Langley Green Road. The road outside it was lowered to give additional headroom under the neighbouring railway bridge and steps had to be made up to it. According to Leslie Frost in the "Oldbury Weekly News": "probably the best known licensee of the Railway Tavern was Freddy Weldon,

who had played for Aston Villa and was actually a member of the team which won The Double - the League Championship and the Cup in 1897". It ceased to be a public house just before the outbreak of the Great War, when it was purchased for the Zion Church, Langley Green Sunday School extension programme.

taken from the "Oldbury Weekly News"

The Old Cross

Langley Green Cycling Club outside the Old Cross ca 1900
Centre of back row S Round, 5th from right C Dyson, 4th from right A Dyson. far right E Williams. Second row far left T W Fanthom, 3rd from left F Butler. Front row 2nd from right S H Cross.

A somewhat later photograph of the Old Cross Inn, showing Mr Marygold (who lived in Farm Road) with his pony and trap

The Royal Oak

A very early photograph of the Royal Oak in Langley Green

Temperance

Not everyone frequented the local inns and taverns. Indeed some members of the community were firmly opposed to strong drink.

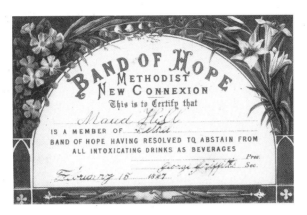

An abstinence card from the Bethel Chapel dated 1887

Langley Temperance Hall, known as "The Institute"

The Institute was built as a Temperance Hall in 1875 and was managed by a committee. In about 1876 the Langley Literary and Debating Society was started and in 1877 Mr J E Wilson of Albright & Wilson presented about 1000 books to the society, to form a library. This library was free to all members, numbering then over 100, and to all persons living or working within a radius of two miles. A few years later, due to increasing membership, the committee had the Temperance Hall enlarged and additional Club Rooms were built. This led to a further increase in membership and operas including "HMS Pinafore" were performed. The name of the society was altered to the Langley Club and Institute and their committee took over the management of the whole building.

In 1894 the new Reading Room was opened to the public and the Institute's lending library, replenished by Mr Charles Showell issued books on Wednesday evenings only! In 1896 the Langley Institute Library was taken over by the Oldbury Urban District Council and became a public library.

information taken from Oldbury Urban District Council annual reports

Langley Hall

In 1988 Langley Hall, "located on the corner of Joinings Bank and Langley Road", came up for sale. It was described in the sales particulars as "a spacious Grade II listed building ripe for improvement and modernisation". With 7 bedrooms and 4 reception rooms, the asking price was in excess of £175,000.

Mr P J Drury, Inspector of Historic Buildings for English Heritage, carried out an inspection in May 1988:

"It seems likely that Langley Hall originated in or by the late Medieval period, and that it was enlarged by the construction of two symmetrical wings in the 17th or early 18th century. It is not altogether clear whether the wings were timber-framed or brick. A number of 6-panel doors with raised and fielded panels and some other joinery in the house suggest a general modernisation, at least of the interior, in the early-mid 18th century. The house seems to have taken on its present appearance during a progressive re-construction probably in the 1830s ... By the time the central range was rebuilt in the early 19th century, an upper floor had probably been inserted, and indeed, parts of the framing of this appear to survive ... The central block was clearly timber-framed."

taken from the sales particulars and the inspector's report

Chapter Two
1900 - 1919

Warley Institutional Church: origins

Warley Wesleyan Methodist Church had been established in George Road for fifty years when some of the young members wanted freedom to work out the practical and social side of their Christian faith. To avoid friction with older members, they started to meet separately, and Warley Institutional Church came into being.

The first meeting was held in a field, the in Pound Road in April 1906. By 22nd April they had rented land, re-erected an old wooden building, converted it into a church and held the first services in "Warley Institute".

Working party 1906

They did not immediately use the word "Church", but by 1912 it was becoming known as "Warley Institutional Church". Nevertheless, in 1913 they were sued for non-payment of rates by Oldbury Council, who claimed that they were not a church and therefore not exempt!

They soon purchased the land, and much work was carried out by members extending the building and laying out facilities for football, cricket, tennis, croquet and bowls.

1907 - the first building

By 1910 it had a singing class and an orchestra of 30 players, and various study classes, including the "Mutual Improvement Class", which provided weekly lectures and debates on religious, social and general themes. It was a centre for worship, recreation, debate and action on social issues of the day, its aim being "... the Spiritual and Social good of all who care to join us ..."

Plans were made to erect a larger brick building, but the first World War delayed this. Within five years a very active fellowship had been established under the leadership of G Norman Robbins, Harry Dearne and John Goode. Many of its members were involved in the social and political development of the area, and it established pacifism, temperance, education and social justice as cornerstones of its practical Christian message. By 1910 it accommodated 140 people, and the average Sunday School attendance in 1913 was 176 pupils!

Terry Daniels

Sunday School Processions

These were a major event in the calendar. Children were always immaculately dressed, the girls wearing special white dresses, often their only new dress in the year.

Sunday school procession on the occasion of George V's Coronation in 1911. Seen here coming up Langley High Street to Uncle Ben's Bridge, with Langley Park in the background.

Zion, Langley Green, procession in Station Road at the corner with Mill Lane 1911. Note Showell's Brewery in the background - in January 1905 they were advertising Showell's Ale in the "Weekly News" for 2/- per dozen pints.

Edward Street Methodist Church Sunday School anniversary procession 1912 in Station Road near the level crossing; led by founder members Leonard Hull & son Leonard and George Henry Griffiths (far left).

Benjamin Southwick Winwood, one of the leaders of Edward Street Church, was choirmaster and trained children for the anniversary. When he was tragically killed in a traffic accident, Beryl Taylor took over.

Zion, Rood End, anniversary procession 1912 in Vicarage Road, looking towards the Merrivale from where the traffic lights are now

51

Zion Church, Langley Sunday School Extension Scheme

The third Chapel & cottages. The cottages were demolished in 1913 for the widening of Langley Green Road. To the far right, set back from the cottages you can just see part of the "Railway Tavern" building, which ceased to be a public house just before the outbreak of World War I.

An extension fund was started in 1908, as a result of the Sunday School Teachers asking the Deacons for more room for scholars. There were excellent congregations and the Zion at the beginning of this century was full by 5.55pm. Pew rentals and family pews were in operation - a source of revenue, and difficulty.

On the side of the chapel nearest Langley stood the old "Railway Tavern" and a cottage belonging to Holders Brewery. Almost in front were two cottages occupied by the Russell and Sheldon families, these were the property of the chapel. The Tavern and cottage were bought from Sir John Holder for £300. Part of the land was sold for £160 for road widening and with a donation from Sir William Albright and others the purchase price was soon realised.

Under the leadership of Mr E W Jackson, plans for the Sunday School extension were made and work soon progressed. The cottages were demolished, part of the public house was converted into a house for the chapel's caretaker, and the school building finished.

Zion United Reformed Church

Sunday School foundation stone laying

Rood End Schools 1906

In 1903 Chance's Schools, which belonged to a firm who were "the pioneers to a certain extent of education in Oldbury", were closed and temporary provision had to be made. The council was also called upon to close the Free Schools and, in place of those two schools, the Rood End Schools were opened on 26th July 1906 by Mr W A Albright (due to the ill health of Mr J W Wilson).

The accommodation for 627 children was provided in two departments. The Mixed Department was designed with two separate entrances for boys and girls respectively, so that the department would be "capable of being worked as a two department school". The Infants Department consisted of two classrooms and a schoolroom, being divided into two by a moveable folding partition. It also boasted a "marching hall for the drilling of infants under cover". The desks were "of the most up to date pattern, the top forming a book rest, while a separate shaped seat is provided for each pupil".

At the official opening the "ample classrooms" and "excellent assembly hall" were highly praised, but above all the "magnificent playground", where the children could enjoy the light and sun, which were "unfortunately all too often absent in such manufacturing districts", although the speaker stressed that the smoke cloud was a necessary product of Oldbury's industrial prosperity.

taken from the "Smethwick Weekly News" 28th July 1906

Titford Road Schools 1911

On 8th March 1911 the schools in Titford Road, Langley were officially opened by Mr G S Albright. The architect presented Mr Albright with an inscribed silver key as a memento of the occasion. The total cost of the buildings, including furniture and fittings, was £14,500 and the schools housed 1,016 children. It was the first school in Oldbury to have three separate departments (infants, boys & girls, each with a separate central hall) and the first to have a Cookery Centre.

The Headmaster was Mr C C Robbins, the Headmistress of the Girls' Department Miss E Tomlinson and the Headmistress of the Infants' Mrs P Round.

from "Smethwick Weekly News" 11th March 1911

Langley Free Library

Built in 1908 on land supplied by Mitchell & Butler's Brewery with £1,500 towards the cost supplied by Andrew Carnegie, the new Carnegie Library in Barrs Street, Langley was formally opened on 26th February 1909. As Mr A M Chance was ill and unable to perform the opening ceremony, Mr W A Albright officiated. Attendance was affected by the severe weather and the usual formality of unlocking the main door as part of the ceremony was dispensed with owing to the persistent downfall of snow. The Chairman, Mr J Gill commented "Such libraries afford to the labouring poor an opportunity of acquainting themselves with what is going on throughout the world by means of newspapers placed at their disposal in comfortable reading rooms, well warmed and well lighted". The civic dignitaries and leading businessmen invited to the official opening rounded off the proceedings with tea at St. Michaels' Schools.

from "Smethwick Weekly News" February 1909.

The Old Navigation Inn

My father Charles Edward Etheridge was born in the Old Navigation Inn in Titford Road in 1901. His father, Charles Etheridge, owned the pub and brewed his own beer.

I remember my father telling me how miners from a local mine were paid their wages in the pub, but his mother always refused to serve them until they had taken money home to their wives.

Nancy Adams (née Etheridge)

A Oakes, the family department store

The family business was established in 1905, its first premises being in Barker Street, Rood End.

In 1910 my grandfather William Oakes, a builder by profession, built the whole corner block, which includes our present premises, numbers 174 to 180 Vicarage Road. He also built a number of other properties in the area including some in Richmond Hill.

The first Oakes shop in Vicarage Road was built for his wife Ada, who was a milliner, hence "A Oakes". William Oakes died in 1916, when all his six sons were quite young and the shop and rent from some other properties were thus my grandmother's only source of income. My father, Frank Oakes, was only six, when his father died. His mother told him that, when his father was building the shop, he used to say that it would be the new replacement shopping centre for Oldbury town.

Robert Oakes

M Round, drapers

Ada Oakes was one of several sisters, who all learned different trades. Her sister, Minnie Round, went into drapery and opened a draper's shop in Langley Green Road.

When Langley Green was redeveloped about twenty years ago and the buildings between the corner of Edward Street and the corner of Henry Street were demolished, the family business moved down to Langley High Street, where it was a well known feature until the business finally closed about ten years ago.

Robert Oakes

Wincott, the butchers

Wincott's butchers shop in High Street Langley. The young butcher's boy in the picture was sadly killed in the Great War

As a young man my father William Wincott, being the eldest son, worked the butchers shops up, one by one, for his younger brothers. He really was too gentle and sensitive to be a butcher and was always upset when he had to start killing the first of the spring lambs and could never eat that day. It was very hard work handling the hind quarters of beef etc. My grandfather, Mr Solomon Wincott of Oldbury, was a hard taskmaster and would say: "Now, come along boys, back to work. I don't begrudge you your food, but I do begrudge you your time!" The animals came up from the country by train and the drovers took them from the station to the slaughter house behind the shop in Langley.

57

My father moved from the Langley shop to Langley Green, where Chris Gunn came to us as a lad of twelve and in later years took over the shop.

Mera Newey (née Wincott)

The Albright & Wilson Fire Brigade

Originally formed to combat the ever-present danger from Zeppelins, the Albright & Wilson Fire Brigade still exists. It is a leading member of the Sandwell & District Industrial Fire Brigade Association. In addition to providing a professional fire service within the Works, the Fire Brigade hosts competitions each year attended by brigades from all over the country.

Tom Tomlinson

A fire brigade trip. Samuel Alfred Aston, standing in the front row wearing a bowler hat, was seconded from the fitting shop to be the first motor mechanic for Albright & Wilsons.

I remember my dad coming home from work and studying late into the night. He was a trained fitter, but as a mechanic he was largely self taught.

Win Round (née Aston)

Katy's Arm

My nan, Katy Hale, was born in 1897. On leaving school at the age of 12 she went "into service". The hours were long - from dawn till dusk; the first job of the day was lighting the cooking range. Katy's only time off was one afternoon a month and there would be jobs to do when she returned from those few hours of freedom.

During World War I, young women were being encouraged to help the war effort and after being presented with a kipper for her Christmas dinner by a well-known, wealthy Langley family she walked out and got a job on munitions. This was in 1916. Katy's new job was testing hand grenade detonators at Albright & Wilson. The tester held the grenade upright, crooked her arm upwards, then bent over forwards, gently immersing the shell in a tank of water. If bubbles rose upwards then it was faulty and declared "leakage"; these were put into a neutralising tank.

The girls all got on very well and soon became good friends. They were proud to be helping "our lads". One fateful day Katy was caught on the left elbow by a "leakage shell", which exploded on impact. The works medical volunteers acted swiftly, applying first aid and then packed her off to hospital. Katy stubbornly refused to allow the amputation of the damaged half of her arm.

There was no Health Service then. Albright & Wilson offered to organise experimental surgery to try to save her arm. They offered her the choice of a lump sum to cover her medical bills, or regular payments over so many years - Katy chose the first option.

Some of the doctors who carried out the operation were not British; one was a Chinese surgeon, another was what we would call a physiotherapist today and she may have been Swedish or Norwegian. The shattered elbow was replaced with an almost rigid artificial one made of metal. Tubes were inserted to replace destroyed major blood vessels, then the severed halves were carefully re-joined.

Katy found the movement of her arm was permanently restricted afterwards, but at least she still had her arm. As a child the dramatic events made a great impact on me each time Nan told the story of her arm. The silver scar that almost circled her arm never looked too bad to me, the circular scars each side of the elbow were more impressive. I recall how Nan would try to pose her arm so it didn't look "too gammy" as she would say - especially if anyone was taking photographs.

When I asked her why everyone else who was so badly injured in the war wasn't mended like her, Nan would always say she had been a very lucky girl. In her 70s Katy had a stroke, and it was obvious the doctors had not believed that anyone had the technology to re-connect limbs so long ago - until they saw her x-rays that is, when they were most interested to learn how it had been done!

Katy Hale died in 1977 aged 79.

Verna Hale Gibbons

The Women's War Medal 1914-1918

Phosphorus when burnt gives off a very dense smoke. During the very early days of the 1914-1918 war, the tactical importance of efficient smoke screens was soon realised.

Albright & Wilson at Oldbury were experts at making phosphorus - and soon became experts in making devices for generating smoke on the battlefield. "Chinese tumblers" and "Plum puddings" were two such devices.

Phosphorus liberated by a small detonation, produced opaque clouds of phosphorus pentoxide. This masked the enemy fire and, being non-poisonous, allowed our own men to advance without great discomfort. It is recorded that the first use of this kind of device in the history of warfare was at the battle of Loos.

One great change which resulted from the war effort was the employment of women and girls in the factories. From about 550 people employed by Albright & Wilson in 1910, the payroll increased to almost 1,000 during the war. Well over half the total may be assumed to be women and girls.

At the end of the Great War a farewell concert was held at the Institute Hall in Langley - Mrs Bate, the supervisor presided over the concert given by the girls themselves.

Each of the ladies received a war medal struck by Albright & Wilson. Few of the medals seem to have survived. One, however, is cherished by the family of Katy Hale and another is retained in the Company archives as a reminder of a massive war effort by local women.

Tom Tomlinson

Katy's medal

Warley Institutional Church: challenge of war

The 1914-1918 war was the first real test for the newly-formed Warley Institutional Church and its pacifist stand. Its statement of belief asserted that "... the taking of human life was contrary to the will of God". Some members did join up, and several were killed in action. But many registered as conscientious objectors and appeared before local tribunals. Some were exempted, some were imprisoned and others were sent to work on the land or into the army. With the men away, much of the running of the church passed to the women.

The Church campaigned actively against the war, and started a long association with the Fellowship of Reconciliation.

Terry Daniels

Warley Institutional Church, Senior Group 1917

War Widow

My grandmother Kitty Gilbert (Louisa's daughter, see Chapter One), worked doing washing and cleaning to support her family of six children when her husband was killed in 1916 at the battle of the Somme. The gardener at Langley Hall used to bring the doctor's washing down to her house in Henry Street.

She was the person neighbours would send for when anyone died, as she would do the laying out. She would also be there to help with the births.

My father told me that they had to go to school sometimes without any breakfast, until she had earned some money. Then she would give them their food through the railings at playtime. Often he had no shoes to wear at all, or had to make do with a clog on one foot and a pump on the other.

Barbara Powell

Kitty Gilbert at the back of her house, 40 Henry Street

Starting School

Class 1C St Michael's School around this time.

Emily Tranter (née Vincent) started school at St. Michael's in 1916:

So there I was at the school door in my corduroy dress and my little button boots. That school, St. Michael's, was to be my only place of education and I would stay there until Christmas 1924. I was in a class of about forty boys and girls. Stiff backed as ramrods we sat at straight rows of dark wooden desks on hard, bench-like seats. Each desk top had its own ink well, which would be filled regularly by some of the more reliable lads.

We weren't allowed to use our voices in class except when chanting our "tables", reciting poetry or singing. Our teacher had a cure for talkers; a sharp rap across the knuckles with the ruler. If this didn't do the trick then the cane was always at hand.

Emily Tranter (née Vincent)

The Canting Patch

Locally "canting" described those lengthy chats, gossips or "chinwags" indulged in by our grandmothers, mothers, aunts etc when they got together.

Popping next door for a "borrow" and a gossip was a necessary and therapeutic part of the housewife's daily pattern. Those women did not go out to work, but stayed at home devoting their whole lives to domestic tasks - and what hard drudgery some of those tasks were! The links between the women were strong and reliable. They weren't rivals but friends, sisters in the struggles and hardships of life.

Canting wasn't a quick snatch of talk made with one eye on the clock, but a leisurely and satisfying experience. No wonder husbands described it as being a "canting session".

And where would this gossiping take place? Why, just inside the door of the "back" room, of course! Arms folded comfortably, each woman would lean against the wall touching it with her arms and hips. And how the talk would flow!

Had there been only paper, the wall would soon have become discoloured, as each day's canting was followed by another and another. However, this painted patch was just the job. It could easily be wiped down and given a new "lick" of paint.

So there you have it - the Canting Patch. The place where those women, who were the heart of our family life, met to grumble about husband, children and the cost of living; to compare ailments and share old remedies and old wives' tales; to experience mutual comfort and closeness in times of sorrow.

Wilfred Tranter

Langley & District League

In March 1919 the Barrel Bowling Club with its president Mr A C Watson held its annual general meeting at the "Barrel" Inn.

Other bowling clubs in the fixtures list for the league this month included the "Hen & Chickens".

from "Smethwick Weekly News" 14th March 1919

Alfred Hands, pork butcher

In March 1919 the "Weekly News" reported the death of Alfred Hands, who had been a pork butcher for over thirty years, churchwarden at Holy Trinity Church for twelve years and was "a man of genial and upright character".

from "Smethwick Weekly News" 7th March 1919

Alfred Hands' shop at Langley Green

The Peace Celebrations 1919

Peace Celebrations in Langley Park 1919

I remember the Peace Celebrations. I was just nine at the time. My friend Rene Fulford, aged 12, daughter of the park keeper, is sitting at the front of the picture in a white dress. We went to the church service in Langley Park and then in the evening we went up to Barnford Hill for the fireworks and bonfire - bonfires have never be allowed in Langley Park because it's so small. I remember a kind young man, Mr Watts, letting me sit on his shoulders so that I could see what was going on.

Evelyn Wood

The same Peace Celebrations in Langley Park showing the Bandstand

"The celebrations in the Langley Ward commenced with a united thanksgiving service in Langley Park ... In the afternoon sports were held at Barnford Hill.

"In the evening about 350 old people of 65 years and upwards were entertained to dinner in the Zion Congregational School, Langley Green.

"In consequence of the rain it was decided to postpone the fireworks display and bonfire on Barnford Hill, but the latter was subsequently lighted and formed a fine spectacle."

"The Rood End and Tat Bank district was profusely decorated, and processions of children, masquerading in fancy costumes with decorated vehicles, were formed. Mr S. Whale, coal merchant, had several finely decorated lorries which aroused much interest."

"Children's Day in the Langley Ward was certainly the star feature of the local peace festivities. The parents had taken especial interest in the event, and most of the children were in fancy costumes, with the result that the procession of school children through the principal streets, headed by the Langley Prize Band, formed a most interesting and picturesque spectacle.

"The procession assembled in Langley Park, where massed singing took place accompanied by the Prize Band.

"After the happy ceremony in the park the children were entertained to tea and in the evening sports took place in the cricket field, Crosswells Road.

"The day's festivities concluded with a bonfire at Barnford Hill and a firework display, the effectiveness of which aroused much enthusiasm."

from the "Smethwick Weekly News" 25th July 1919

The Oldbury Book of Memory

The Oldbury Book of Memory is housed in its own display case in Langley Library. It is removed only for the Remembrance Day Services each year and for the occasional addition of a missing name. One page is carefully turned at regular intervals.

The inscription reads:

"Herein are inscribed the names and regiments of the men of Oldbury in the County of Worcestershire who fell in the Great War 1914-1918.

"This record forms part of the town War Memorial and is intended to be preserved for all time as a token of gratitude to, and remembrance of, those who laid down their lives in the time of their Country's need".

The pages contain the engrossed names, ranks and regiments of the fallen, whilst at the end of each letter are left spaces for the names of other fellow-townsmen who made the supreme sacrifice but whose names have not yet been recorded in the book owing to lack of information.

Chapter Three
The Twenties

Old Park Lane, Langley in the 1920s

My family lived in Brades Village till I was seven, when they moved to a new house in Bristnall Hall Lane. My grandparents, John and Sarah Howen lived in Old Park Lane, Langley and I often took myself to visit them. In those days children weren't worried about being "took off" and I was a real roamer. At the age of 5 or 6 I once went to the pictures in Oldbury, went exploring for a short cut home and ended up getting lost in Langley. Suddenly a voice called out "It's Billy's lad!" It was Jack Hale, my Aunty Kate's husband, whose parents lived at 31 Broad Street, Langley. Jack took me back to Brades Village none the worse for my adventures.

Not long after we moved from there my mother, Nellie, was taken seriously ill, so some of us kids went to stay with our grandparents at Old Park Lane. Granddad was a big chap, 16 stone and well over 6 foot tall. Granny was a little, thin woman, I think she was Welsh. I spent a few months with them during the summer of 1925. It was like paradise with so many things to keep me occupied. They lived in one of a row of four old cottages set well back from the Lane, other Howens lived in the other three. I recall how big the front gardens were. They went right down to an open brook of clear water, which ran in front of the little terrace and carried on along Park Lane.

Parts of the brook were culverted over and houses were built over these sections. I remember the cottage gardens were always full of flowers. My grandparents lived in the end cottage, a well used footpath passed by it with the brook running under it. This path went through open fields past the big Marl Holes left by clay mining and it lead up to Birchfield Lane. There was a wooden stile you had to climb over at that end. There was plenty of room for horse and carts to go along it as far as the stile, I should think it was about twelve feet wide.

At the back of the terrace was a large yard of blue cobble bricks, where there were always chickens running around. Surrounding the yard were the "outhouses", sheds, pigsties and pigeon lofts. I think Alf Barnett owned the pigeons.

There was a quaint little footbridge with wooden railings round it, leading from Old Park Lane to the other end of the cottages. I spent many happy hours wandering through the fields and got to know which plants and berries were safe to eat. Sometimes I followed the brook up to the Blue Billy waste heap - when you watched you could see the chemicals discolouring the clear water. I had a good friend, one of the Fanthoms. We once volunteered to take a horse to the blacksmith's up that way, we loved any excuse to watch him working. Other times we used to sneak past the watchman and take shovels to dig out caves on the slopes that were big enough for five of us to hide in. That chemical waste stood firmer than soil, it never needed propping up to stop it collapsing. It's all gone now - except the brook, they've built a new Industrial Estate there.

When the weather was hot a gang of us lads would go swimming in the cut. There's many a good swimmer who learned to swim that way in those days. Of course, playing along the canal banks was another great favourite as a pastime. There were lots of barges to wave to and climb aboard then.

One of the things I always dreaded was trying to avoid the geese someone kept up by Blue Billy. They used to run down an entry and try to attack us as we passed by, and one big white one was particularly vicious - it nipped many a leg and bottom, but he never got me!

Bill Howen

Mr Bill Howen died in February 1997. These memories, as told to his cousin Verna Gibbons, are published with the kind permission of his family.

The Blacksmith

Although motor transport was starting to make its presence felt in the 20s, and especially the 30s, there was still a considerable amount of horse transport, and all needing attention. Thus, we had our very own local farrier in Langley village, and his name was George Thomas - Thomas the blacksmith to us all. He lived in Titford Road just across from the church, and his smithy was on a piece of ground where Old Park Lane runs into Park Lane, backing on to the little "Blue Billy". I never saw him in anything but his working clothes to be honest, with his split leather apron and old trilby hat, but he was such a familiar figure toddling up from his forge to the "Model" to slake his thirst with a half of Frederick Smith's. He always seemed to walk in the middle of the road, it was as though he denied that there were such things as motor vehicles.

Bill Hipkiss

Hooves in the street

For forty years there was a slow clip clop of horses hooves down Titford Road, past Holy Trinity Church and into Trinity Street (the "Oxford") to the phosphorus works of Albright & Wilson. Four times a day they journeyed to and from the stables on the corner of Titford Road and Broad Street, at 7.25, 12.35, 1.25 and 5.05, regular as clockwork to those who lived on the route. Then during the day there was the clip clop of the horses carrying industrial waste of various sorts from the works to the tip between Titford Road and Birchfield Lane.

Chemical waste was transported in the heavy steel "mud-cart". This had to be moved carefully so that it would not spill on the roadway. One particular grey mare had been trained to pull this cart very slowly and steadily, skilfully placing one foot in front of the other to avoid rocking the cart.

These were the horses of "Cockbill and Sons, Hauliers", who operated from stables at 16 Titford Road in the centre of Langley. George Cockbill started the haulage business after moving with his family from Wick near Pershore in the 1850s. However, it was his son Joseph, and Joseph's four boys, who developed the business until they had a dozen or so horses, ran their own smithy in Park Lane, and had a dairy business delivering milk from a pony and trap in the area.

So, their business was not limited to industrial waste. They also ran horse-drawn buses between Langley and Oldbury, especially popular on Saturday evenings when produce was being sold off cheaply at Oldbury market! They owned smart landaus and provided a horse-drawn taxi service as well.

The business lasted from the late 19th century until the early 30s, when Joseph died. Unlike many other carters, the Cockbills did not move into lorry haulage, but stayed faithful to horse power right until the firm closed.

Compiled from memories of the Cockbill family and inhabitants of Langley by Terry Daniels

One of Cockbill's carts outside the Sycamore Inn in Clay Lane

The Milk

In the 20s milk was delivered from outside the area in bottles, but we had our own "milk-men" in the vicinity, Hodgekiss and Wooliscroft, and they sold milk "loose" from churns. The Hodgekisses lived in Titford Road just a few doors from George Thomas, but I don't remember them on their round, perhaps they left us to the Wooliscrofts who lived in Old Park Lane.

With Polly, his daughter, Mr Wooliscroft used to come round with a pony and small cart stacked with milk-churns and other produce, butter, eggs, and such. To accommodate all this the tail-gate had to be down flat, and they would drive away standing on this - as a child I always expected the poor little pony to be hoisted off the ground.

Bill Hipkiss

Harvesting ca 1924 at the junction of what is now Farm Road and Pound Road

The "Royal Oak" Public House

The Butler family were a very well known wealthy family in Langley Green in the early 1900s. One of eleven children, Ada Smith (née Butler) owned the "Royal Oak", which sold Holders Ales. She was so well known that a visit to the "Royal Oak" was usually described locally as "going to Ada's". When she sold out to Mitchell & Butlers, her brother Fred Butler became manager of the pub and Arthur Davis, his brother-in-law came to assist him.

76

Gertie Billington was the barmaid for several years and later married Fred Butler. Arthur Davis married Floss Butler and I used to look after their son Sam. My job was to make sure that he stayed out of the bar and was clean and tidy, as his dad was very strict. I was only ten myself. At fourteen I left school and had to start earning money. I went to the World's Wear Sewing Factory in Oldbury, but I can't say I enjoyed the work much. As a trainee I only earned eight shillings a week, so my dad let me leave and I moved on to Parkes's Confectionery.

Elsie Cartwright (née Hadley)

Sam Davis with his uncle Fred Butler, taken in the grounds of the Old Cross Bowling Green ca 1927

Warley Institutional Church: social witness

In the 20s, the members of the Church set about strengthening the fellowship again and constructing a more fitting building. Foundation stones were laid in 1924 and the building opened in March 1925 (see below).

The seven stones in the front wall of the church set out the vision of the Church: *Service, Education, Social Justice, Peace, Reconciliation, Temperance, Fellowship*. The next year, local miners involved in the lock-out associated with the general strike were employed to lay out the grounds (see below).

The years between the wars were the ones where the Church was most involved in social developments. In 1921 it set up a "Communal Scheme" for its members, whereby those taking part paid in according to their income and circumstances (single, married, number of children etc). They then drew out when they needed money because of sickness, unemployment or unexpected need. By 1933 the scheme had 56 members, and it operated until 1950.

Many Labour members of Oldbury Council were associated with the Church as the drive for social justice continued. Three Mayors of Oldbury, Bernard T Robbins, John F Goode and Ruby Starkie, were long-time members of the Church. The meeting room was used by Oldbury Council as a welfare clinic for four years until it opened Bleakhouse Clinic.

It was involved in temperance work, opposing the erection of licensed premises in the area. In 1927 it resolved that "... this Church strongly disapproves of the action of Oldbury Council in granting permission for the sale of refreshments in the Parks on Sunday and requests the Council to institute a referendum ..." In 1936 it petitioned against the Sunday opening of cinemas.

Terry Daniels

Causeway Green Methodist Chapel

William Parkes, son of the builder of the church, was born in 1857. He was the pillar of the church in his day, starting in the Sunday School as a young lad and eventually becoming the superintendent. In his later years he served the community as a JP, but his heart and soul was in the little chapel at Causeway Green. His life's work revolved around the church and after his death in 1925 many believed that the church would rapidly lose its active membership and that closure would follow. How wrong they were.

Electricity finally came to the chapel in 1927 and was installed by one of the members, Mr W Shipstone. A new heating system and a new pipe organ (the present one) had been installed in 1912 at a final cost of £280. Half of the total cost was raised by sewing meetings, garden parties, sales of work etc and half was donated by the Carnegie Trust.

The organ was built by Henry Hewins, Organ Builder, Stratford upon Avon. A young man working with the organ builders during the installation took it upon himself to maintain the organ on behalf of the builders. He remained faithful to his task until he retired in the late 50s. His name was Percy Parris and his name was recently discovered carved neatly onto the top of the organ bellows. The organist from 1909 until 1961 was Mr H Hadley.

In 1928 the old iron schoolroom was purchased second-hand from a Miss Holland of Oldbury at a cost of £52. A bargain when one thinks of the many events, meetings, socials and celebrations which have taken place in that building over the 53 years that it served. It was originally a school and the men of the church dismantled it on site. It was transported to Causeway Green and assembled behind the church. When it was finished the men's' labours were rewarded by the ladies with a lavish cooked dinner. Roast pork, apple sauce, beef and tongue being on the menu. A good feed at Causeway Green seems to be tradition.l. Sadly, but inevitably, the old school was demolished in 1981 to make way for our new church centre.

John Hadley

Community involvement

Throughout this period the churches provided the majority of the social activities in the area. Congregations were much larger than today and numerous football clubs, drama groups, choirs etc. were formed.

Zion, Langley Green Football Club

Zion, Langley Green Church Football Club
Bill Blewer, Frank Lewis & Clem Good are among those shown

The Langley Bethel Chapel Cricket Team

I was a follower of the team in the late 20s, but much too young to play, though I did eventually take on the job of "scorer" Our home ground was behind the "Queen's Head", Londonderry, but we did once go as far as Buckingham to play. The team continued well into the 30s, but I became otherwise involved on Saturdays.

I remember names of those who played over a period: Tom Beard, Alf Binfield, Eddy Hammond, Bill Lewis, Harry Love, Cyril and perhaps Wilf Partington, Howard and Les Pullinger, David Smallwood Snr, Harry Withers and, last but not least, Walter Picken, who was the Sunday School Superintendent and later the local preacher - and a useful member of the team at that. There were others whose names now escape me.

Bill Hipkiss

Langley Bethel Chapel Guild Cricket Club

The Merry Reds

The formation of this group was the idea of Albert Roberts and Les Pullinger. Mr England played the piano. The Pullinger family kept a cake shop in Barrs Street.

The group was formed in about 1927 and lasted for three or four years. All of the members attended Edward

82

Street Chapel. The concerts consisted of popular songs of the time, monologues, sketches, etc, with performances being given at local chapels.

Win Round (née Aston)

The Merry Reds from Edward Street Methodist Church 1929 in their distinctive red and white costumes. Front seated: left Millie Hall , right Rose Pullinger (née Newby) Centre row from left: Amy? Gardener, Agnes Taylor, Wilf England, Beryl Taylor, Win Round (née Aston). Back row from left: Howard Pullinger, Edna Hall, Les Pullinger, Doris Blewitt, John Ruddall, Hilda England

Edward Street Women's Own

Edward Street Church Women's Own 1920s (which nowadays continues as the Ladies' Fellowship) Mrs Harold (3rd from left in back row) had a shop at 55 Farm Road. Mrs Griffin (6th from left, 2nd row from back) kept a greengrocer's three doors away from Mrs Harold)

Langley Green Zion Amateur Operatic Society

The Operetta "Aladdin" performed in the Sunday School at the Zion, Langley Green in 1927 or 1929

I remember sitting in the front row with other children to watch, it was all very exciting. The leading role was taken by Mr Albert Aston, who had a fine tenor voice. On Albert's right is Mrs Evelyn Clay, who had a beautiful contralto voice, on the left is Miss Tilly Lewis who took a leading role. On Mrs Clay's right is Mr George Smith who had a fine baritone voice. The other names I can identify are Mr Gerald Smith, Mr Harry Bowater, Miss Evelyn Lewis, my own two sisters and my father Sam Round (2nd from right in second row) who helped with the scenery.

Vera Round

Spring Street Choir

Spring Street Methodist Church Choir

Sunday School

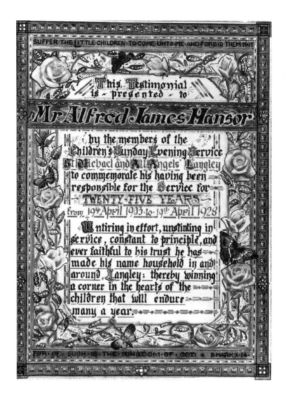

St Michael & All Angels Sunday School testimonial presented to Alfred James Hansor in 1928 for 25 years service.

The County High School

The first secondary school in Oldbury was started in premises at Flash Road, shared with the technical school. It was a mixed school, unusual for that time, and catered for sixty pupil teachers and forty-nine secondary pupils when it opened in 1904. The school expanded over the next twenty years until it outgrew the buildings and facilities in Oldbury.

In 1926 the school moved to a new building in Moat Road, then still a "green-field" site, and so into the Langley area. The cost, £37,000, had been raised by the county authority, and so it became the "County High School".

The facilities for the 320 pupils better than those at Flash Road. In 1927 an unheated, open-air swimming pool was provided by G S Albright. However, it was next to Matty's Farm, and before the grounds were fenced in 1934 stray sheep and cattle had to be driven off the fields before games. The corridors between classrooms were open to the elements, so that in the worst weather rooms were so cold that pupils had to wear overcoats.

Terry Daniels

The County High School in Moat Road, Langley - later Oldbury Grammar

Sewing Lesson - Rood End School 1925

Beyond the age of ten, and it was while I was in Miss French's class, there was one lesson which I heartily disliked. For one

87

hour during the week the class was separated. The boys of whom there must have been about twenty were sent into the playground for football. The girls remained inside for sewing. Each one had her own special garment to work on, every stitch having to be done by hand. My particular item was a white callico petticoat and I had mastered and completed, under tuition of course, the french seams needed at each side, not, I may add, to the entire satisfaction of Miss French herself.

The afternoon arrived when I was to begin the hemming all round the bottom. Miss French had pressed the item to the required depth, started me off with half-a-dozen very fine almost invisible stitches, stressing that I watched her closely. On passing the garment back to me she remarked on its becoming soiled from too much pressure of hot fingers and was quick to point out several tiny red spots which the fabric had soaked up from pricked fingers. She ended her cutting rebuke with the comment that good laundering would be necessary before the garment could be worn.

I returned to my seat trying in desperation to match the small even stitches begun for me as an example. My hands became hot, the needle sticky and the cotton damp through undoing and re-threading several times. I was back where I had started. Hate was seething within my breast.

Miss French was only four or five desks away on her inspection round and soon she would be on top of me. Wildly and at break-neck speed I thrust the needle a full inch ahead securing the hem, another jab and another, each stitch gaining in width on its predecessor. Almost in a matter of seconds I was half-way round just as the dreaded inspection arrived. Quickly my handiwork was removed from my clutch. Then, fixing her steely gaze upon me and emphasising every syllable I heard

"This is dis-grace-ful. Take it at once and show it to the Head Master and tell him I've sent you".

With cheeks the colour of beetroot I slid out of my seat, head bent, my gaze rivetted to the ground, aware that all eyes followed my progress to the door until I disappeared through it. Slowly I walked up the corridor, glanced at the clock on the wall in the empty hall and reaching Mr Olden's door on which was the awesome title "HEADMASTER", knocked. Timidly I remember, for I heard no sound from within. Repeating the tap, a loud "Come In" bade me enter and I stepped inside.

The headmaster sat with a pile of books before him and looking at me over the top of his spectacles said

"Well, what is it?"

Mr Olden had a very bristly moustache. All my male relatives, with the exception of my grandfather, were clean-shaven. Consequently, men who displayed a hairy growth on the face and particularly on the upper lip, were regarded as decidedly old.

"Please, sir", I ventured, "Miss French has sent me to show you this", and I held out my work which he clumsily took from me.

He pressed his lips together until his moustache completely covered his lower lip.

"Hem" he said, and a second longer drawn out "Hemmmm" issued forth. Then,

"Well, v-e-r-y, nice, very nice. Now, run along I'm very busy".

"Thank you, sir", I answered and escaped as quickly as I could hardly believing my good fortune.

No enquiry was made on my return for the sewing lesson had drawn to a close and everything was put away for another week.

Miss G L Brant

Rood End School and the War Memorial commemorating those lost in the Great War. The Memorial was made by Mr Dallow of Blackheath and was unveiled on 19th March 1921 by J W Wilson (of Albright & Wilson). There was a procession of clergy, forces, and Langley Prize Band headed by Bandmaster, Mr GHill, followed by Master Joseph Dickens attired as a sailor boy bearing a Union Jack at Half-Mast. The Memorial is made of Aberdeen Grey Granite, bears the title "Pro Patria Mori" and cost a total of £160.

A Typical Village School

Causeway Green School in Pound Road was about halfway between the Wolverhampton Road and the corner of Brook Road. It afterwards became a Conservative Club until it became part of the college car park.

It was a church school, connected with St. Paul's, Long Lane, Blackheath. We would walk there at Easter, Christmas

90

and other special days for a service. It was quite an old school. I started there in 1921 at the age of four and left in 1932 to go to St. Michael's.

There were only four classes, it was such a small school. I can still remember the names of the staff: headmaster - Mr Hensman; teachers - Mrs Butler, Miss Rickers, Mr Bricknal and Mr Downing. We sat on wooden benches in front of a long table furnished with the usual ink-wells, and the only heating was a rather large round stove in the middle for the smoke to get away through the roof; it was only lit in winter of course, and on very cold days the stove-door would be opened for extra heat.

At the side of the school was the caretakers' house, a Mr & Mrs Rose: Mr Rose was a first-aid man, and fully able to attend to any small accidents that sometimes occurred. There was a plot at the back of the school that was used to teach the boys gardening, and our sports-ground was a field at the rear of the "Barrel" pub.

Discipline was strict, one teacher, Mr Bricknal, used a cane cut from a beech tree that grew in the grounds; I can see him now whittling it down to his liking. One teacher was riding his old, sit-up-and-beg bicycle one day when a particularly cheeky boy said, "Isn't your wife washing today, sir, as you have the mangle out?" This earned him a hundred "lines" every playtime for a week.

Hilda Broadbent

Around the area
On the other side of the road was a large house that was once a pub. I don't remember it being used as such, but the sign was still there, it was called "The Saving Hand" and the landlady

was a Mrs Mary Ann Thomson. I can remember quite a large family living there, and their name was Potter. In front of it was a wooden shed from which they sold sweets, ice-cream and the like. On the site of this old pub in Pound Road now stands quite a large detached house.

A little further down lived Alfie Clift the woodman, who would tour the district with his horse and cart selling his firewood. He was such a character, most unkempt, not to say scruffy, but my father took pity on him and insisted that my mother invited him in for a cup of tea when he called; this she duly did, having first placed a rough, old chair near the door. He would usually begin by taking off his boots and rearranging the rags that he wore round his feet instead of socks, then he would take his cup of tea, pour it into the saucer and noisily slurp it up. Mother was most pleased - when he went.

Across from the "Hen & Chickens", about where the Wolverhampton Road runs now, was Bilter (Bill) Hadley, who had horses and carts etc. Father was very fond of horses and he would often hire one, with perhaps a brake, or a brougham, and take us and grandmother, and maybe a neighbour or two, and we usually went to relatives at Hunnington, or perhaps the "Sun" pub. It seemed to be quite a good day out then - and we enjoyed it.

Hilda Broadbent

Tiny Brook and the Bard of Pound Road

As you go down the "little" Pound Road from the Wolverhampton Road, Brook Road is the first turning on your left, and it gets its name from "Tiny Brook", which ran along behind the present houses and doctor's surgery in Pound Road, part of which is still there behind the Barrel Pub. Brook Road was a lane up until about the late 30s, and there was a small bridge across that brook.

From the far corner of that lane ran a row of eight houses called, not surprisingly, "Eight House Row"; in between where those houses finished and the "Barrel" was an old cottage that lay back from the road, about where the surgery is now. In that cottage lived Jim Bastable, who was quite a musician and pianist, writing several pieces of music and songs, which he used to play and sing in the various pubs and clubs in the area. Two of those songs were; "Where The Avon Flows" and "Where The Severn Wends Its Way" .

My friend Bessie Bennett (née Rose) lived in the last house in Eight House Row as a child and can remember her father coming home from work in the quarries and going over for a drink at the "Saving Hand".

Hilda Broadbent

Dyson's Mission, Langley Green Road

The Langley Green Mission was founded in the late 1920s by Mr Edward Dyson in memory of his wife. With the help of the firm - Messrs. Simpson & Co - the building was erected on land belonging to the Great Western Railway and adjacent to the railway on the far side of the railway bridge in Langley Green Road.

The building, of wooden construction, was furnished inside on the Non-Conformist lines and the services were conducted by a certain Mr Harry Storey, who was at the time Welfare Officer for the Simpson Rolling Mills, which had two Works - one in Park Lane adjacent to Albright & Wilson's and one in Freeth Street, Oldbury.

As far as I can remember, services were held twice a week on Tuesday and Thursday evenings. My grandparents on my father's side, together with their daughter and her husband, were members from its inception - my Aunt Kate played the harmonium for all the services. She, and other ladies who attended, formed a women's class which used to meet in an afternoon.

At some time in its life the building was used by the St. John's Ambulance Brigade as their headquarters - my grandfather and my father were both members at that time.

I cannot remember the full details leading up to the closure of the Mission, but the harmonium ended its life with my Aunt Kate in Old Park Lane, Langley.

John Bridge

Local Entertainment, Twenties-style

The Holy Trinity School building was a centre of activity for social events in the years before the radio took over in the 30s. There were concerts and plays by local talent, and what were just known as "social evenings". In addition there were the usual groups such as Scouts and Guides, Church Lads Brigade and just plain clubs with all sorts of things going on. Bonnie Bill, son of the landlord of the "Model", gave a lot of his time to these activities, and George Weston, son of the High Street greengrocer, was involved in the Cubs and Scouts.

In the late 20s the building was also used as a day-centre for the unemployed, where there was instruction in useful crafts such as carpentry and shoe repairs. A new curate at the time was the Rev. Povah, retired major (Indian Army), and as most of the unemployed were ex-servicemen he took a particular interest in them. About this time the then Duke of

Kent paid a visit to the centre. The Rev. Povah later became vicar of St. Mark's, Londonderry.

All the above activities were replicated in several other religious institutions in the area, but I was more involved in the events at Holy Trinity. I did take part in gramophone recitals in the Bethel Sunday School, where turns were taken in supplying the music; hardly anyone had transport, and so this meant lugging the gramophone and records all the way up to Whyley Street - this was where I came into it sometimes.

Bill Hipkiss

Values

How wonderful to be able to buy a loaf or a bag of sugar for 4d, a bottle of milk for 2d. A short back-and-sides, a pint of beer, 10 best cigarettes and a decent seat at the cinema all of those for 2/- altogether. Wonderful that is, until you realise that the average *skilled* man would only earn 1/3 per hour. A little arithmetic and you will realise that those prices were no more friendly than they are today - most of them less so.

Bill Hipkiss

Washdays in Junction Street

Mondays were terrible, hard, long days in homes of the 1920s and 30s. It was "washday" for most housewives, but meals and other chores still had to be done as well.

The laundry was done in a separate small building at the rear of the house, the brew-house. This housed the shallow sink, boiler, mangle, wash tub, wash board, dolly etc. Mondays first task (ca 6am) was to light the coal fire under the water boiler in the brew-house. The deep copper bowl of the boiler was set flush in the tiled brickwork, with its bottom in the fire and a wooden lid covering its open top.

There was no running hot water, no electricity, rubber gloves or washing powders. Water was hand scooped from the copper into the tub, soap shaved from the bar onto the clothes in the tub and the wooden dolly was then used to agitate the wet clothes - a back breaking job. A garment with stubborn dirt would also have to be rubbed on a soapy wash board and, if this failed, boiled in the copper. After this there was still the rinsing and mangling to do!

The day was still not done until the hung-out clothes were dry enough and had been ironed. The flat irons were heated over the fire. Two were rotated as they became too cool to press the garment. Then there was just the cleaning up, putting away and digging out of the fire ashes!

Patricia Rickers (née Bury)

Miss Katy's School

It was a private school in Bloxcidge Street for girls only, when it was started by Miss Katy's mother, but by the 1920s when I went there it was mixed. Miss Katy, trained only by her mother, ran it with the help of a trained teacher. We may not have been taught much science etc, but the "3 Rs" were very evident, along with more genteel things like country dancing and needlework. Several pupils made it to the Grammar School in Moat Road.

Margaret Shaw (née Millinchip)

96

Miss Katy's School in Bloxcidge Street

The New Wolverhampton Road

The new road was officially opened on 2nd November 1927 by the Prince of Wales.

About two to three thousand people turned out to give him an enthusiastic welcome at the junction of the new road and Causeway Green Road. For the great occasion the "Hen & Chickens" Hotel had been gaily decorated with flags and bunting, and at night coloured electric lights were lit all around the building. From Causeway Green Road to Jarvis Bridge the road was lined workpeople from the neighbouring factories, and on the bridge itself hundreds had congregated making only a very narrow way for the cars to pass.

from the "Weekly News"

Langley Carnival

Langley was famous for its carnival when "Jonathan" roasted an ox. One year Pearl Underhill was Amy Johnson, complete with a model aeroplane in the parade.

Margaret Shaw (née Millinchip)

Pearl Underhill as Amy Johnson outside the Langley Institute

Quarefellows at the "Merrivale"

This men's club was started by Stan Darby, Mr Nixon and Mr Snade. There were dances every month and Christmas dinners and these were always held at the "Merrivale" public house.

Florence Hadley

The "Old Cross" Bowling Team

The Jackson Shield is a bowling trophy that hangs in the "Old Cross" lounge. It was donated to the bowling club by William Jackson in 1918 and is still played for every year. The names of the first eleven winners are on the shield.

Trevor Ford

98

Unknown opponents with the "Old Cross" bowling team (right). My father Sam Snade stands at the back just right of the trophy.

Langley Maltings

Langley Maltings were originally owned by Showells and the buildings date from the 1890s. They overlook the Titford Canal and the grain was originally brought in my the boats of Fellows, Morton and Clayton. In the 20s the Maltings caught fire. I awoke in the night and looked out of our window and saw the flames leaping out of the roofs. I remember there being several fire engines. Next to these buildings were the four large fuel tanks of the Shell Mex yard and my father was called out to help move several rail tankers in the sidings over the road. It was a very dangerous situation. I remember the distinct smell of burning malt for several days afterwards!

A V Baker

The Pictures

The "Regent" in Crosswells Road began life as the "Cinema". My mother took me there to see Charlie Chaplin and Jackie Coogan, but especially to see Rudolf Valentino in "The

99

Sheik". I don't remember the film because I was very young and was probably there only to keep her anchored to reality - he had a tremendous effect on all the women.

As I grew older I joined the crowd at the "Snob". One old penny on Saturday afternoons and Wednesdays after school. All the films were silent then, but all the big girls read the captions off the screen for the benefit of the younger ones, or to show off their reading. We sat on hard benches and the projection room was just a shed-like affair at the back - and made a terrible clicking noise.

But it had its day at the beginning of 1934 when the cinema was refurbished and became the "Regent" - sound had been there for a while, and now it was sophistication and opulence beyond our dreams.

Bill Hipkiss

John Laister, violinist

John Laister was my neighbour in Arden Grove. He survived the 1906 San Francisco earthquake, in which his father was killed, and returned home to his mother in Langley. He was the second man in Langley to volunteer when the First World War broke out. He was a self-taught violinist, who worked with Jack Judge, and has just celebrated his 100th birthday.

Florence Hadley

Chapter Four
The Thirties

The World of Work

The area still benefited from farmland, existing side by side with local industry:-

Langley from "Judbury" Hill (now part of Barnford Hill Park).
It has been suggested that "Judbury" (or "Jugbury") is a local corruption of "Jubilee".

Harvest, Causeway Green Estate 1934

A tower at Albright & Wilson's felled Easter Monday 1932

The Arden Knitwear Co.

Staff from "Arden Knitwear" in Arden Grove in the early 30s

I worked for Arden Knitwear along with a number of other local girls. We produced really high quality clothing and supplied Harrods, Selfridges, Marshall & Snelgrove, John Lewis and Dickens & Jones, as well as some of the up-market shops in Birmingham. The business moved from Langley into Birmingham in the 30s, to Hall Street opposite the General Hospital. I left in 1942 because of a bomb and came back to work at Myers.

Nancy Jones

Lather-Boy...

In December 1933 I left school at fourteen and started work for Archie Connop, the barber in High Street, Langley; the job description was "lather-boy", and I held that post for three months.

Quite a few men went to the barber for a shave then, which was done with an open razor, a fearsome tool really. All that I was allowed to do was to apply the lather, and then the soap had to be well massaged into the chin to soften the bristles.

When Archie had done his job, mine was to sponge and dry the gentleman's face, and perhaps, if not too much blood had been spilt, receive a tip. I must say that my boss very rarely nicked a customer.

I did other little jobs also, like sweeping the floor, brushing men down before they left, and keeping the Brylcreem dispenser filled. I was just getting to use the new-fangled electric clippers when I left.

... and the "Starter-upperer"

What I found the most interesting, even exciting part of that job at the barber's was not inside the shop. He had an Austin Seven, and he was proud of it - well, apart from Mr Fox the outfitter, and Westons with their greengrocer's van there were no more vehicles in the street as a rule.

There was only one problem for Archie - no self-starter on that model; that was where I came in. Almost the first thing he did was introduce me to the mysteries of a rather complicated procedure; turning on the petrol and tickling the carburettor was just the beginning. Check the gears, retard the ignition, pull out the bit of wire that was the choke and turn the handle a few turns, now switch on. This time the thumb had to be kept out of the way in case the handle kicked back as it was cranked - that thumb, if not the wrist, could easily be broken.

Then, if all had been done properly, it might start; that would make Archie happy, I would be as proud as Punch, and off he would go somewhere, and I would plaster my hair with Brylcreem or such like.

Bill Hipkiss

Walter Hughes, Pawnbroker

A well known figure in Broad Street was Mr Hughes, standing at the doorway of his shop with his black apron on. The shop was opened at eight a.m. and a fire lit in the back room, and many of the regulars made use of this to sit and cant. One woman came in just after eight and at about ten-thirty she suddenly remembered the egg she'd left boiling, she'd been so happy canting. There was one woman who started to come in every Friday to look at the carpet patterns. She said she was only looking for her sister, until Mr Hughes said "I'm very sorry, Madam, but you won't find your sister in there".

Mrs Hughes also ran a pawn shop in Whyley Street.

Millie Smith (née Hughes)

Shops in the High Street, Langley

Greens' was on the corner (with Broad Street), the most exclusive shop in Langley, then came the gully, which ran from Arden Grove into High Street, and was closed off each and every Good Friday by Fred Green, brother of Frank, to prove that it was not really a right of way. Then came Sam Wincott's the butchers, a few more shops and then Mrs Jennings' sweet shop and Slim's the ironmongers next to the Institute. Part of the Institute had been turned into the Gas Showrooms which my late husband, Bert Smith, managed until he went into the R.A.F. at the outbreak of war.

There was a house at the back where Mr & Mrs Wheldon the Institute caretakers lived, he had a false eye and

105

the story went (he told it) that when he went out he would leave it on the mantel-piece to "look after things" for him.

Other shops were Mrs Turner the wool shop, Connop the barber and Billy Weston the greengrocer, whose children Vic, George and Freda helped run the shop.

Millie Smith (née Hughes)

Mr William Ezrah Weston, fruiterer of Langley High Street, with his son Victor in a much earlier vehicle. Taken at the turn of the century at the top of Joinings Bank.

The Master Bakers

My father Zephaniah Russell was a master baker and his shop and bakery was at number 33 High Street, Langley, opposite Langley Park. Nearly every child in Langley must have had a birthday cake made by him and then their wedding cake too. He was well known for his pikelets.

On a Christmas morning he cooked the turkeys and cockerels for customers in his large baking oven, and charged 3d for this service.

Barbara Dunnett (née Russell)

At Xmas the local people took their poultry to be cooked in the baking ovens at the baker's in Langley - behind what is now Mellors shop. At Xmas dinner-time I used to go down with Granddad Healy to collect our fowl. We carried it back home covered with a tea-towel. It was cooked to perfection!

Nancy Adams (née Etheridge)

A Mellor

Marge Rose (née Cockbill) started working for the Mellors at the age of eleven. She found a real interest in shoe repairs and worked for the family until she retired a few years ago. She was one of the few women shoe repairers in the country.

Arthur Mellor established his first shop in Trinity Street in c. 1929, making Mellor's the oldest surviving retail establishment in Langley. He used to make the clogs for the workers at Albright's. Later he moved over the road to larger premises in Trinity Street next to the Newmarket Tavern. When Arthur died in October 1994 the ownership of the shop in Langley High Street passed to me, his son.

Robert Mellor

F P Gaunt & Sons Ltd

Another long established family firm is that of F P Gaunt & Sons, funeral directors, who originated in Blackheath in 1900. The family has played an important part in the Rood End community since 1937.

When Stan and Amy Gaunt were married in 1937, they moved to open a branch office in Vicarage Road, Rood End. As there was no telephone, they had to cross the road to Alex and Nancy Wincotts, the butchers, to use theirs.

In 1955 Amy Gaunt opened the flower department. The office was taken over by Peter and Ann Gaunt in 1966 and continues today.

Peter Gaunt

Parkes's

The next place to have the benefit of my labours was Parkes Classic Confectionery; I was assistant "sugar boiler" to Bill Cutler, who later became a notable town councillor.

My job was to weigh all the ingredients: white sugar, brown sugar and glucose into a copper pan - this must have been at least 20" in diameter, and perhaps 14" deep, with side handles. When the correct measure of water had been added, I'd put it on a gas burner and stir the concoction until it boiled, then transfer it to another jet to carry on boiling at a steady rate for a certain time. I would then prepare the next lot.

Bill would pour the first one on to a heated metal slab when it was ready and proceed to knead it; in the meantime I would be repeating the process. What strikes me now is that as a 14 year old I was allowed to handle such potentially dangerous stuff, in such a relatively large vessel.

The weather became very hot in late May, early June, and with such a warm job we were put on morning shifts, six till two. Not to worry, after three months at Parkes's I was off on my next assignment - a butcher-boy.

Today's teenagers must envy us the way we could flip from one job to another, but they were very often "dead-end" jobs, and an extra couple of years at school would have been a better option.

Bill Hipkiss

Barring-up

I almost forgot, between Connop's and Parkes's I did a stint at M C L, but instead of coming home smelling like a lavender bush, it was now Suds-oil, so the consensus among friends and relations was that I wasn't so welcome as before - how I got myself soaked in the stuff I do not know - and I resigned after one week. In any case I found the work tedious just putting fresh bars in a machine every so often; making little screws as far as I can remember, and the management didn't beg me to stay.

Bill Hipkiss

Langley Green Allotment Association

My mother's father, George Healy was secretary of the Langley Green Allotment Association for a number of years. Every year seed potatoes used to be sent from Scotland to Langley Station for sale to members of the association. They were weighed and sold in what was presumably an old stable next to the Old Cross Inn on Langley Green. I remember going there with him on these occasions.

Nancy Adams (née Etheridge)

1930: The "Cremalt" Year

Jack Judge, writer of the world-famous classic "It's a Long Way to Tipperary" lived in Rood End at 21 Victoria Road from 1928 to 1938, and a great many songs first saw the light of day in that house. After giving up the professional stage in

1921 Jack concentrated on his song-writing, taking on his younger brother Ted and their pianist Jack Jesson as apprentices from 1929 till 1931, whilst Britain was being ravaged by the worsening economic depression. Ahead of his time in many ways, he also turned his creative talents towards advertising, producing catchy jingles that would not be out of place on commercial television today. Towards the end of 1929 the trio worked on "The Cremalt Song" and "I've Been Eating Cremalt" to promote Cremalt sultana maltloaf made by the prize-winning Albion Mills Bakery at Tat Bank Road, Langley. The jingles were aimed towards children, and they were soon skipping along to school singing the nutritional praises of Cremalt. The songs caught on so rapidly that Mr Ellis, the bakery manager, asked Jack to record them. Backed by Jack Jesson and the Blue River Band he gave both the full treatment in typical boisterous style, and before the end of February 1930 the discs were ready for sale on the Piccadilly label, complete with a picture of a packaged Cremalt loaf on either side. They were literally snapped up like hot cakes.

As the economic gloom intensified the children of Rood End were able to escape growing deprivation by their involvement in the Cremalt phenomena, and with the next development excitement levels rose from sky-high to astronomical - the songs were to be used for radio advertising. Sung by a group of professional child singers, their songs, about their Langley cake, as taught to them and recorded by their own local celebrity were being broadcast over the airwaves into their own homes. What blue-skied Halcyon days! Wherever you went in Rood End and the surrounding district that summer, you were guaranteed to hear some youngster singing or playing the Cremalt songs, the world temporarily transformed and glamorous, the "Depression" forgotten as unemployment escalated beyond the previous worst ever figures that August.

The glorious impact of those events left a lasting imprint on many young memories during 1930, those who speak of Jack Judge and the Cremalt experience usually take on a wistful, but happy, far-away look, still able to recall the words and tunes, and always with pride. The Albion Mills Bakery was destined to become a casualty of the Depression a couple of years later, but the malt house emblazoned with the faded CREMALT trademark survived until 1996, when the ruin was further dismantled. Still producing new material, Jack Judge died aged 65 in July 1938, just two weeks after leaving Rood End.

Verna Gibbons, relative of
Jack Judge - an excerpt from her forthcoming biography

Events & Celebrations

In 1934 a "Baby Day" was held in Barnford Hill Park, which would appear to have been very well attended:

1935 saw enormous celebrations for the Silver Jubilee of King George and Queen Mary:

Silver Jubilee Celebrations 1935 in Barnford Hill Park. This culminated in a spectacular firework display with a tableau of the King & Queen's portraits in fireworks.

Street party in Titford Road on the occasion of the 1935 Jubilee

Mr William Gilbert Wood, park keeper at Langley Park, floodlit the Park House to celebrate the Jubilee:

Mr Wood succeeded Mr Fulford as park keeper in August 1934, moving from Bury Hill Park.

Living in Langley Park House

One of the rituals which had to be carried out each week was the winding of the clock in the tower above the Park House. This entailed climbing into the loft and turning a very heavy handle in a limited space. The bell struck every hour, but it did not keep us awake half as much as the stamping noise at Hughes Johnson's works.

When my Dad was on holiday, arrangements had to be made to wind the clock and this was often done by Jack Walden, who was caretaker at the Langley Institute Hall. It was quite a catastrophe for the local people whenever the clock stopped!

My Dad used to grow all the seeds required for borders in the Park in the greenhouses adjacent to the house. The greenhouses were heated by coke and it was my Dad's job at night to go out and stoke the boilers whatever the weather.

Jessie Warkup (Mr Wood's daughter)

Mr Wood by the Park House (now Langley Park Community Centre)

My husband was very proud of the park. He used to grow beautiful roses all along the railings, right up to Uncle Ben's Bridge, and wonderful shows of tulips and daffodils in the spring. He was very upset when the decision was taken for his greenhouses to be demolished and the plants all grown at Barnford Hill Park.

Evelyn Wood

114

A Formal Affair

In 1935 a very formal 21st birthday party was held in the Bethel Church Sunday School in Whyley Street for Miss Edna Griffiths, daughter of Mr Arthur Griffiths of the shoe shop at 16 High Street, Langley (see below). Also on the photograph (in front of the piano) is Frank Griffiths, Edna's brother. He took over the shop when his father retired until his death in 1968.

Isabelle Shepherd

Granny Billington's

The shop on the corner of Henry Street and Edward Street belonged to Granny Billington and was known locally by that name. As my mother had to go to work, I used to call in the shop most days to buy small items, though I was only a child at the time. Granny Billington was a lovely lady. She opened her shop from early morning until late at night, like most shops at that time. Her home was in Henry Street. She owned a meeting house, which was at the back of her home and could be hired for parties etc. She would close the shop at lunchtime, to have her snack and a rest, returning to the shop in the afternoon. She often took me home with her, where I'd receive a cake and a cup of tea. I would sometimes play with her granddaughter Edna.

Granny Billington had a large family, as her husband had eleven sons and she eventually had three daughters - Kate, Bertha and Ada. They would all help their mother in the shop, as they were a close family. Many a local family would have found life harder without their help. All her family were very clever and got to the top of their chosen professions

Granny Billington herself was a great inspiration, for life was hard, yet she always found time to listen, giving her advice when needed. She sold most things from a pin to a bundle of firewood, sweets, candles etc and the world was put to rights over her counter by all the neighbours and friends. Everyone knew what was happening locally round the little streets - who was out at work or off sick. She was greatly missed when her life came to an end and will never be forgotten by all who knew her, as she was such a kind, sweet lady.

Those little streets were full of characters, like Mrs Gilbert in Henry Street, who would come if there had been a death in the family. No waiting for an undertaker, she would lay them out. If there was an illness and washing to be done, there was no one better than Mrs Page of Edward Street. She would do the washing for you, no talk of cost - everyone was in the same boat, they had nothing so would help each other. Times were hard, but you really could rely on your neighbours.

Peggy Cowley (née Lester) formerly of 3 Langley Road

Granny Billington's shop on the corner of Henry Street & Edward Street

Borough Of Oldbury Royal Charter of Incorporation 1935

A petition for a Charter signed by 5,783 inhabitant householders, (out of the total of 7,936 then in the district), was prepared as far back as 1921. The Royal Charter was finally granted by HM King George V on 22 August 1935.

Of the Insignia of Office and Civic Plate, the Mayor's chain and badge was presented by Albright & Wilson; the Mayoress's badge chain with pendant was presented by Chance & Hunt; a silver fruit bowl by Hughes-Johnson Stampings Ltd.; two silver cake dishes by Messrs Ham, Baker & Co. Ltd. and a silver salver by the Langley Forge Co. Ltd.

The Borough of Oldbury Coat of Arms shows a red dragon for Ancient Britain issuing from a Saxon crown. The gold lion upon a green field in the Arms is taken from the coat of Robsart, the distinguished ancient family prominent in the mediaeval history of Oldbury; the cross is that of the Saxon

Kings; and the helmet is an esquire's.   The Motto may be read: "Let it's ancient glory flourish".

information from the Borough of Oldbury Charter Souvenir

The Oldbury Coat of Arms appeared proudly throughout the new borough, although most of them have now disappeared. At least two remain in Langley, metal castings on the main gates of Barnford Hill Park by the park house. I remember admiring them daily in the 50s, as I went past to school. They were about a foot tall and very striking, painted in their correct heraldic colours. Following the borough changes, they were painted over in dark green, but are now back in full, if slightly faded colours.

Terry Daniels

Langley Baths

Official opening by B T Robbins, Mayor of Oldbury. Guests included Ald.. K H Wilson and Ald.. J B Downing, Mayor of Halesowen. They are seen here on the front steps, which were replaced with a new disabled access ramp in 1997.

1937 saw a major event in Langley - the official opening of the Public Baths in Vicarage Road on 8 May. This was a major new facility for Oldbury and one that had been sought for over twenty five years. The Vicarage Road site was selected for its central position in the Oldbury Borough and because of the "relative situation of the various schools".

The Mayor, Bernard T Robbins described swimming as "a most suitable pastime and exercise for persons of all ages, and it is a desirable accomplishment in which everyone should be proficient; and the new facilities will therefore be particularly welcomed by the schools, as swimming will now form part of the curriculum".

from the Official Opening Souvenir

Causeway Green Methodist Chapel

I remember going to Sunday School every Sunday afternoon in the old iron schoolroom. We only lived five doors away. There were picnics on the lawn at the side of the chapel and anniversaries in the chapel, when we sang hymns and took turns to recite poems and quotations from the Bible.

My mother and father were caretakers for a few years. I remember my father getting up early every Sunday morning to light the coke furnace for the chapel and my mother did all the cleaning. My brother and I were expected to help. We used to love going down the steps under the chapel to the stoke hole with our father - we loved the smell of the hot coke and the furnace - but we weren't quite so keen on helping our mother with the dusting!

Derek Bastable

The Christian Party

In 1937 G Norman Robbins, President of Warley Institutional Church, published a programme "Suggestions for a Christian Party". The "Christian Party" was set up locally, but attracted interest from all around the country. Its ambitious aim was to "Work directly for the complete reorganisation of world society on a Christian basis". Its programme covered employment terms and wage levels, a thirty-five hour week, reducing unemployment, redistribution of wealth, restrictions on alcohol (including a complete ban on drink-driving), strengthening the League of Nations, and much more that sounds familiar today. It fielded candidates in local and general elections in Oldbury and other parts of the country. With the changed political situation after the war there was no place for small independent parties, and it was wound up in 1950.

Terry Daniels

Bristnall Hall Farm Housing Development

The Bristnall Hall Farm land around Bristnall Hall Lane and Road, Queens Road and Londonderry Road was probably bought by Albright & Wilson from a Mr Bean in 1917 and acquired by Oldbury U D C between 1921 and 1929. Plans then included a cemetery in the Lane and a school in Queens Road.

Later, according to the plans of 1930, two roads, the Bristnall Hall Farm Housing Estate, a school in Bristnall Hall Lane and the Londonderry Shopping Centre opposite the Queens Head were planned.

At Londonderry, the junction of Londonderry Lane and Queens Road had been bisected by Warley Road in the 1920s and the Dogkennel Lane/Bristnall Hall Road/

120

Londonderry Road extended with Reservoir Road soon after. The short space between the two junctions, split by Albright Road, together with Douglas Road and Reservoir Road gave access to the new council estates - the customers for the shopping centre at the Queens Head.

John Hodgkins

Bristnall Hall School

Bristnall Hall Farm itself stood in Bristnall Hall Road directly opposite its junction with Bristnall Hall Lane. Bristnall Hall School was built on land belonging to the farm, very close to, but not actually on the site of the farm house.

The Moat Farm

The farm house had 2 sitting rooms, larder, kitchen, dairy, 6 bedrooms, 2 closets and a cellar. The farm buildings ranged around a feeding yard, including stabling for 13 horses, a carriage house, cow house, hay barn, geese house and piggeries. There were also two three-roomed cottages in Vicarage Road, presumably for farm hands. According to the particulars, valuable coal measures were believed to underlie the whole of the property.

taken from the Moat Farm sales particulars

Moat Farm and Moat Farm Infants School

Moat Farm Infants School was built on the site of Bristnall Hall Farm. It opened in 1938 and cost £45,000 to build. As Bristnall Hall School had already been established on the grounds of the old Bristnall Hall House, it would have been very confusing to call the new school "Bristnall Hall Farm

121

School", so it was named after another nearby farm - the Moat Farm.

Bristnall Hall Farm Pool 1923 (known locally as Cooper's Farm since the Great War)

The Moat Farm stood just off Matty Road at the place where it joined Defford Drive. It was one of the oldest known places of habitation in Langley. The fashion of building moats was introduced by the Normans after their conquest of 1066 and lasted about 400 years. By the time Henry VIII died in 1547 they had dispensed with moats because they restricted enlargements to houses within them, and the rich and important were well into building massive mansions by then.

A look at old maps of the 1830s reveals there were once many moated properties in the Midlands, but as the population, particularly the rich population, was very small these sites are quite rare nowadays.

After moats fell out of fashion, when most farm land had been successfully drained, they became handy rubbish dumps and gradually they became filled in. The last bit of the

Moat Farm moat was filled in the 1930s, when Defford Drive was built. The last owner of the farm was William Henry Matty, and when the narrow entrance to the farm leading from Moat Lane (Road) was widened and cut-through to join Brookfields Road, it was named Matty Road after him.

The present Infants School was built to cater for children from 5 to 11 years of age; work began on the Junior building when the Infant School was almost complete.

The Infants School opened for pupils to enrol for the new term in August 1938. By that September the building was used as a gas-mask distribution centre. The teachers did all the distributing to the queues and dealt with the paperwork. School was closed to pupils. Teachers issued ration books and identity cards, when they were not filling sandbags.

On 23rd October 1939 the school re-opened to pupils, although attendance was voluntary, not compulsory. Teachers trained the children in the use of gas-masks and how to evacuate the school in event of air raids. On 1st April 1940 school became compulsory again. Until the end of the war there was "frequent interruption to the daily routine" due to enemy air raids.

Verna Gibbons

Thoughts on Moat Farm Schools

Langley was very fortunate to get a model school like Moat Farm, though I think few people now realise it. Designed and built as it was, in the economically depressed 1930s, just before the austerities of the 1940s. We were lucky.

Lucky also with its layout. Its three airy, light, spacious, single storey buildings (Infants, Junior Girls & Junior Boys) occupying a fine, large, sloping site of several terraces.

With such a high class of school I have no doubt that it was staffed to suit. Headmistress Miss Hundlebee and Headmaster Mr Howell and teachers, Mrs Andrews, Mrs Darby, Mrs Steers, Miss Griffith, Miss Jones and Miss Parkes come to mind.

I used to sleep in the classroom when I first went to Moat Farm Infants School. There was a stack of four-year-old sized beds in the classroom. The green or orange canvas was held on green, tubular steel bed frames. The teacher (Mrs Andrews) would spread them out for us to lie down and then keep watch. We had to be still and quiet for about half an hour in the afternoon I think.

In the early days of the war we attended a film show, probably on "Shelter Discipline". The assembly hall full of children let out a shout of glee as we realised that one of the film stars, shown in the Anderson shelter, was our own Mrs Steers.

Londonderry Lad

Sweets after school

We had two shops in Langley Village. One was a General Stores in Old Park Lane, the other a confectioners in Titford Road, opposite the school. Schoolchildren streamed in to buy bubbly gum, Cadburys halfpenny bars, licorice allsorts, humbugs, and most popular of all "podges". Dependent upon the colour "podged" with a small steel "stick", small prizes were won, the coveted one being the gold.

H G Hale

Chapter Five
The Second World War

Thoughts from early wartime

Gas Masks
    Smelly, rubber faced with a pig-like snout of a filter.
Ration Books
    With covers of three colours - Buff, Blue, Green by
    age.
Black-out Curtains
    Thick cloth on wood frames, sometimes left
    permanently up to the window and over doors. ARP
    Wardens knocking and shouting "Put that light out!"
    No street lights. Cars with tiny slits of light from
    headlights. No street signs, removed to
    inconvenience any German paratroops.
Sirens
    The warble of the Alert sending parents running for
    kids, clothes and food. The dash to the shelter. The All
    Clear wail meant being woken up to go back to bed.
Going to bed under the stairs
    The safest place before we had an Air Raid Shelter.
    Being dressed in a "Siren" suit.
Noises
    The Wrum-wrum of Bombers, the crump and shake of
    a distant bomb, the bright lights of Incendiary Bombs,
    the yellower light of buildings on fire, the shouts of
    ARP Wardens. The clank of Shrapnel on the
    entrance.

Collecting
>After a Raid, in streets and fields, jagged lumps of
>metal, Shrapnel probably from Anti-Aircraft shells
>and white, flat bits, said to be from aeroplanes.

Shelters
>Silver, corrugated iron buried in the garden. Public
>ones, like upturned pie dishes on corner waste ground.
>With bunks in tiers, of wood and steel strips, a
>chimney-like escape hatch at the far (dark) end, smelly
>toilet tin.

Static Water Tanks
>Tall concrete, low steel meant for fire engine pumps
>to dip hoses into to quell fires, but ideal for sailing
>paper ships in. Buckets of sand (for incendiaries) and
>water, definitely not to be played with wherever
>found.

Pipes in gutter.
>Six inch diameter steel pipe with flanged joint laid in
>the gutter (near the Merrivale Pub), emergency water
>supplies, possibly from Crosswells bore holes.

Stirrup Pumps.
>Foot on base, end in bucket (of water), work handle
>straight up and down to squirt water through a "garden
>hose" pipe to dowse a fire.

School closed
>Had to go to nearby private house, front room, with
>seven or eight others some mornings, a teacher came
>to set a lesson.

Barrage Balloons
>Great silver roundish things with three wings at tail
>(very like a bomb, but hugely bigger), winched up
>from school fields, with trailing wires to cut aeroplane

126

wings. Sometimes seen like ghostly spaceships in light
of fires.
Tinned fruit.
A Christmas treat, tinned pineapple cut into square
chunks. In the pantry, eggs in murky preserving
liquid, which didn't always work.

John Hodgkins

Memories of Causeway Green

Early in 1939 my family moved from Rood End to a newly
built house right at the top of Grafton Road. In those days the
area was not developed as it is today and Grafton Road itself
came to an abrupt end a few yards past our house. After this it
became just a country lane with open farm land on the right
and a brook and tall hedge on the left. At the top of the lane
was a wooden stile over which if you turned left you crossed a
wooden plank over the brook and found yourself on the edge
of the golf links. Turning right over the stile you crossed more
open land, which led eventually to Hurst Green or "The
Dumps" as we called it.

Exactly opposite our houses on land now occupied by
Grafton Lodge, was a farm owned by a Mr Swindler (or
Swingler) and during the war as part of the war effort he kept
a lot of pigs. The smell from this pig farm during the summer
months, to say nothing of the huge black flies, was something
not to be forgotten.

The fields behind our houses were also cultivated
during the war and used to grow wheat. After the harvest,
when the wheat had been bundled into sheaves, we children
used to stack them up in a row and play in them like a
wigwam.

The local school for us was Holt Road at Blackheath. We used to walk from the top of Grafton Road, down Woodnorton Road and across the corner, which is now the motorway bridge, and all up Cakemore Road (which we called "The BTH" road, named after the factory at the top; now called Electromobile). At the island we turned left and then along Nimmings Road to Holt Road; quite a long walk for little 5 year old legs!

Audrey Taylor

I remember the war years ...

I was born in Church Street, Oldbury, but my family moved to live in Jarvis Crescent, Langley on August 26th 1939 - just a week before World War II was declared on September 3rd 1939 - I was eight years old.

Both of my parents were ARP (Air Raid Precautions) Wardens - my mum, Mrs Lois Kenny, was a full-time warden and was based at the Langley Institute. I spent quite a lot of time there with her, during her duty shifts.

I remember the other wardens based there:- Mr Everest of Joinings Bank, Mr Norris the photographer whose shop was in High Street Langley, Mr Miller and Mr Dolman both from the Grafton Road area in Causeway Green, Miss Winifred Castle of Jarvis Crescent. The Equipment Officer at the Institute was Councillor "Harry" Price, who also served a term as Mayor of Oldbury.

The Institute stored emergency supplies, foodstuffs, first-aid, gas masks etc, all in readiness in case of air-raid disasters. There was also a team of first-aid ladies on duty shifts - they sometimes "borrowed" me as a practise patient, bandaging and splinting me to test their skills.

Next door to the Institute (probably part of the Institute building) was the gas showroom, which had a connecting door to one of the duty rooms. The manager of the showroom was Mr Bert Smith, son-in-law of Mr Hughes, the pawnbroker in Broad Street, Langley.

Several local school teachers did voluntary civil defence shifts at the Institute. I remember a Mr Coll, who eventually became Headmaster at Moat Farm School. He bought me the "Film Fun" comic every week.

Mr & Mrs Jack Weldon were resident caretakers and lived in a house at the back of the main building. Mrs Weldon made lovely leek broth - I often had a warming bowlful on cold winter's days.

From 1939 to 1942 I was a pupil at Titford Road Junior Girls School. The Headteacher then was Miss Bertha Williams from Moat Road. I remember going to a garden party at her home in aid of "Warships Week". Other teachers were Miss Cotton (later Mrs White), Miss Croft, Miss Read and Miss Taylor, who married Mr Ellery from St. Michael's (he was sadly killed on active service in the army). Mr Franks was the school caretaker and lived in the school house. I don't remember any girls who were not a little scared of his wrath, when we ran up his "coke mountain", scattering it all around the playground. The poor man spent hours trying to keep the place tidy.

From 1942 to 1945 I attended St Michael's Senior School. The Headmaster was Mr Orgill (or "Jotter" as he was otherwise known, as he was always muttering "Just jot that down"). He had a very sharp knuckle and if he caught anyone misbehaving he would prod your arm with it, saying "Pray boy (or girl) what do you think you are doing?" His bark was worse than his bite though - he was really quite kind and

129

extremely proud of his "old Boys - or Girls" in the Armed Forces. He would read their letters out to the school in assembly. His favourite publication was "The Listener" (BBC) and excerpts from it were often part of his assembly chat. I remember the names of all the teachers when I was a pupil, but probably the one most people would remember was Mr "Dicky" Bird, who taught Maths and Science for a very long time at St. Michael's.

Our education at that time was interrupted by air-raids - both in daytime, when we had to sit on benches in cold, damp, brick shelters in the playground, and at night-time, when the raids disturbed our sleep and made us tired at school next day. Of course we were in trouble if we forgot to carry our gas masks to school every day! To make up for lost hours we went to Saturday morning school at Titford Road. During the height of the most frequent night air-raids, I slept alone in an Anderson shelter with just my dog "Tony" for company. All my family were "on duty" during raids - I was just 10 years old!

Langley had a "village" atmosphere and it was quite a happy time for me, in spite of the restrictions imposed by the war. I remember people being very caring and helpful to each other then.

I lived by the canal side, so there were pleasant walks along the towpath to Titford Lake, via Jarvis Bridge. We fished for "Jack Bannocks" in the canal. Quite often children fell in - my mum frequently had to bath and dry-out children who had been too daring. One winter evening at around 11pm, my eldest brother was returning home from a works dance, as he started along the towpath (a short cut to our garden), he heard cries for help. The canal was partially frozen over and my brother pulled a shivering man out of the icy water. The man had "taken a wrong turn" after leaving the Navigation Inn and, in the blackout, had fallen into the canal!

At the end of the war in 1945 we held a street party to celebrate Victory in Europe (VE Day). My mum made "fancy dress" for about 30 children in the crescent. To say "thank you" they bought her a china teapot - I still own that teapot, it brings back many happy memories.

Pat Rodwell

War Time

During the war children were encouraged to buy National Savings stamps at 6d and 1/- and certificates at 2/6, 5/-, 10/- and £1 through their school. Stamps could be exchanged for certificates which carried interest. Both could be stuck into suitable books, which were provided by the post office. Those for certificates had a light blue cover.

The teacher would take the money and make up a list of what was required. Stamps had to be stuck in neatly, on the proper page and the right way round; certificates had to go in serial number order. Quite a task with impatient ten year olds.

One day I had been asked to take the money and the buying list down to the post office. I had left Moat Farm School by the top gate and was dawdling down past the sand pits to the post office. In 1944 it was in an old cottage at the corner of Pound Road and Moat Road, opposite the Plough Inn.

Floating in the air and blowing about among the railings and in the gutters were many long strips of metal, one side a bright silver. I collected a few to play with and to take home. Many months later we realised that it could have been a trial drop of the radar-misleading "chaf", used during the D-Day landings.

The route home from Moat Farm School to Londonderry was via Pryor Road, but the *best* way was down Brookfields and, eventually, up Reservoir Road. This was due to the cart track (now Matty Road), which led to that area of adventure and exploration - "The Springies" (Springfields).

The middle third of the track to Moat Road was a concrete-faced dam. This held a vaguely triangular pool in a large field running up to Moat Farm School/Moore Crescent. The watershed was a heavy bog of rushes and reeds and "bottomless" pools. There were moorhens and ducks and occasionally swans or geese on the pool with midges, shiny blue dragonflies and huge brown ones, and moths and butterflies above. We fished for tadpoles, minnows and red patched sticklebacks.

The other side of the dam was a steep bank down to a very large rough field between Brookfields Road and Defford Drive (now the Tudor Road estate). A stream wriggled down towards Langley Baths through a wide strip of bog. The field was very rough with a few patches of good grass and many of nettles. Excellent for adventuring and for war games. In the west side, in 1943, there were several piles of bricks, heavily overgrown, perhaps the remains of the old Moat Farm outbuildings.

Towards the end of the war and for a time afterwards youngsters of 11 to 13 years would roam the district (the school leaving age was 14 and would soon be 15). Their parents were not thought uncaring or to be taking much of a risk. With friends we roamed the area from West Smethwick Park to Barnford Hill Park and from Low Town to Warley Woods, and even further on a Saturday morning. We would cross the Wolverhampton New Road to see an episode of "Flash Gordon" or "Zorro" at the Warley Odeon. We rarely got home with more than scratches or a bruise.

An exception to this was the descent of Manor Road hill. Our "Hong Kong" (4 pram wheels, 3 planks and a big bolt) got into a speed wobble. We overturned at the entrance to the Londonderry Playing Fields. (The gates and railings had gone, together with those of many other parks, schools and public buildings to be melted down for the war effort). We walked home dazed and short of some skin on hands and knees - at our age short trousers were still worn.

The best "Hong Kong" run started from Hilltop, by the little old school building now the "Beeches" pub, then past Coopers Farm, the Baptist Church, the Merrivale Inn and over the level crossing through Langley to the Seven Stars Bridge. It was a long walk back. The passenger's job was to jump off and push along the flat bits. Then, as speed picked up, return and use his boots as part of the braking system.

We could do almost as we pleased on the roads, traffic was so light and slow and petrol rationed. On the main roads we had to mind pedestrians, the occasional bus and a few lorries. On side roads we played football (with an old tennis ball, referred to as "the pill") and other games for hours on end, with only the odd delivery vehicle (cart) interfering.

Horse drawn carts were a source of income, to spend on fruit or a comic, as sweets were rationed. Dogkennel Lane, Warley Road and around the "Two Brewers" pub were good collection areas. We sold the buckets of horse manure we had collected at the big, older, private houses.

Londonderry Lad

Albright & Wilson 1939-1945 and "Don't be a G'awpus!"

In 1939 white phosphorus was being produced at Albright & Wilson sites at Oldbury and Widnes. An enormous increase in demand for the element came from the major war effort. Luke Hadley's Farm on the boundary of the A & W Oldbury Works was taken over by the Government (Ministry of Munitions) who built a battery of six furnaces.

The total cost was £500,000. Things moved very quickly in wartime. Production started on New Year's Day 1940 - just one year after the first sod had been turned on Luke Hadley's Farm.

By 1942 shipping restrictions led to a shortage of phosphate rock. A & W were asked to convert the furnaces to produce ferrosilicon - another material in great wartime demand. In addition to the furnaces (housed in a structure which can still be seen), a series of massive storage silos were erected. They held a total of 23,000 tons of phosphate rock and were 120 feet high. Whilst half of the phosphorus produced in the early years of the war went to munitions, the remainder went to make phosphoric acid, phosphates and other essential compounds for food hygiene and medical products.

An interesting research product in the early years of the war was to produce a synthetic substitute for balsa wood in aeroplane construction. German submarine activity made import of the timber very difficult. Albright & Wilson developed lightweight boards from foamed calcium alginate. It did the work of balsa but was not put fully to the test as the anti-submarine campaign became successful.

Albright & Wilson products were helping to save lives at sea! Flares based on the use of calcium phosphide were produced in their thousands. Marine marker devices, white smoke candles, torpedo indicating lights and lifebuoy lights of a high quality were manufactured to exacting specifications.

The Oldbury Works had its own Air Raid Precaution Service and later its own Home Guard. Both operated under the eye of a senior engineer - George King. A works notice from George states in no uncertain terms:

"DON'T BE A G'AWPUS
Recent Air Raids have revealed a curious interpretation of "Working after the Siren". Groups of men - and women - collected to gawp at puffs of smoke from A.A. guns. The Management's instructions are clear - if you want to work during the alert - and the Management agreed-
then WORK!
If not, you must go to your permanent shelter. To gather in groups and gawp is asking for trouble, and as ARP. Officer I warn you that we cannot take the risk of having so many casualties as this grouping may give from A(nti)A(ircraft) shell splinters".

It seems that the notice worked very well. People either worked on or sheltered. Gawping was a thing of the past.

Tom Tomlinson

Signs of the Times - from the Black-out Days of the Second World War

Trinity Street, which once passed through the middle of A & W Oldbury Works, was once a busy thoroughfare for both pedestrians, cars and lorries. The roadway was bounded by walls on either side for most of its length.

Come the Second World War and a strict blackout was imposed on the A & W Works and all surrounding roads. Armed guards were placed at each end of Trinity Street! Only specially authorised vehicles were allowed to pass and then only under the strictest black-out.

White lines were painted on the walls on each side of the road. These markers assisted drivers to make a safe passage through the street in pitch darkness. Certain sections of the wall still bear these specific reminders of the Second World War and the black-out in Trinity Street.

Trinity Street was always known to local people as the "Oxford". That name derives from the Oxford Engine Works, which stood in Trinity Street at the turn of the century.

Tom Tomlinson

Langley Park

During the war there were four air raid shelters in the park, which were used to the full by the local residents. The RAF also manned a barrage balloon in the park.

Jessie Warkup (née Wood)

The Gas Mask Queue

In early 1939 there were vast queues at Titford Road School for gas masks. As we were waiting an Oldbury Gas Works van drove past me, with the slogan *"Be modern - use more gas"*.

Cyril Forrest

136

Home Guard

Members of the Home Guard ca1940

Entertainment of Wounded Servicemen 1944

St. Michael's Youth Club with the wounded servicemen, Sept. 1944

137

"On Saturday, 30th September, thirty-two wounded servicemen from Barnsley Hall Emergency Hospital were the guests of the members of St Michael's Youth Service Club at their Head Quarters at Titford Road Schools. They arrived at 3.15pm and were very soon doing full justice to the meal provided. It was a very merry meal indeed, the radiogram was in great demand and many requests were received for Bing Crosby records and the "Ink Spots". This formed a bond immediately between guests and hosts as "Bing" and the "Ink Spots" are firm favourites with the majority of Club members. Much amusement was also caused when a number of the girls insisted upon writing each soldiers name on small labels and attaching it to their "hospital blue". This they explained was to avoid confusion... Time passed all too quickly and after refreshments had been served, the festivities were brought to a close with the singing of "Auld Lang Syne". Upon their departure each soldier was given a parcel containing articles which it is hoped would prove useful to them, and were speeded on their way with sincere wishes for a quick recovery".

article from Langley Parish Magazine courtesy of Doris Pierce

Warley Institutional Church - pacifist witness

Warley Institutional Church pursued its opposition to war, and supported the Peace Pledge Union, War Resisters International and the Fellowship of Reconciliation. In the late 30s it petitioned against compulsory gas mask and air raid drill, opposed its fencing being removed by the Ministry of Works & Planning to make armaments (and won!), and declined to assist in ARP work.

As in 1914, when war came, some members joined up, but others went to prison or joined local rescue squads. As part of its work on reconciliation, the Church made contact with local prisoners of war.

During the war, the Christian Party set up a "Communal Scheme" on part of the church grounds to provide work for conscientious objectors. The main activity was the sale of produce from a nursery and greenhouses on the site. After the war, the scheme was discontinued and the Church must have been the only religious organisation in Langley running a commercial nursery! In the early 50s it was leased out, and finally sold to Messrs Harris & Sons, greengrocers of Cape Hill.

Terry Daniels

Founder members in front of the greenhouses ca 1948

Childhood Memories

I remember the Italian Prisoners of War laying the hardcore for the section of Farm Road from Leahouse to Pound Road. They made us ships in bottles.

Brian Jones

Grow More Food Campaign demonstration plots in Barnford Hill Park 1940

Horticultural Show, Langley Baths, Vicarage Road in 1945 in aid of the Red Cross and St. John's Ambulance, when £188 was raised.

The First Aid Post

The First Aid Post and ARP Ambulance, taken on the car park at the back of the Langley Baths

I was one of the volunteers and worked shifts there. There were huts fitted up for the treatment of casualties and where we could sleep.

They used to have dances at the Baths then and we would very often go to the dance first, before we started work. I remember Mr Morgan, who was in charge of the Baths - he was always very kind to us. I decided after a while to become a nurse and left to work at West Bromwich Hospital the night they bombed Coventry.

Naomi Lewis

New Years Eve 1940

New Years Eve Dance at Albright & Wilson Recreation Club 1940

The Anderson Shelter

I remember waking up in the middle of the night, aged four or five, to find myself being carried up the garden path to the air raid shelter by my father, with the sound of the sirens wailing.

My sister would already be in the shelter, completely inside a gas mask designed for small babies, with my mother beside her, nervously smoking a cigarette. For some reason no front doors were supplied as part of the air raid shelter kit. For the first few nights we just had a roll of old linoleum.

Michael Cox

The Sunday School Christmas Party

Bethel Chapel Sunday School Christmas Party 1944

The mothers always provided the refreshments for the Bethel Christmas parties - we had jelly, salmon and shrimp paste sandwiches and cake. In the war time the mothers saved up their rations and all helped out.

The minister in the picture is Rev. Crossland. To the far left is Mr Bayliss, the Sunday School Superintendent, who ran the Sunday School for a number of years. On the minister's left is Eric Dawes - he provided the entertainment at the Christmas parties, showing black and white cine films of Charlie Chaplin and the like.

Brenda Salisbury (née Cockbill)

Fragnoli's Ice Cream

Giuseppe Fragnoli's shop in Rood End - taken just after the war. In the picture are his daughters Annie (back), Teresa (left) & Louisa (right). Louisa's pinafore dress was made out of a new grey army blanket by Mrs Baxter, the tailoress who lived at 102 Barker Street.

Giuseppe Fragnoli came to Birmingham from Italy at the age of twelve and was an ice cream maker in Smethwick before he moved to Barker Street. He had an ice cream round in the Oldbury area. The house, 8 Barker Street, was turned into a general stores in 1934, when his health began to suffer

At the beginning of the war customers would queue for ice cream at the shed at the back of the shop, where the ice cream was made. As rationing increased you just couldn't get hold of the ingredients for such a luxury food and we had to stop making it until the end of the war. All of us helped in the shop, serving and washing up, but Dad did everything to do with the ice cream making, originally all by hand - it was a big day when electricity was installed.

We supplied ice cream for several VE parties - he used to make up gallons of ice cream for parties, packed in ice and salt.

Teresa Jaynes & Louisa Nash (née Fragnoli)

Guiseppe Fragnoli otherwise known as "Ice cream Jack"

Fragnoli's ice cream, home-made from a secret Italian recipe, was the best I have ever tasted. He used to come around the streets with an ornate little cart, drawn by a pony.

At that time, we had a pet (Manchester terrier) dog, called Tony. He had a passion for "Jack's" ice cream and drove my mum crazy when he heard the "ice cream bell" ringing. She used to wrap a halfpenny in a screw of newspaper and the dog would carry it in his mouth to the cart, where one of the children would hand it up for him and hand the halfpenny cornet back down to the eagerly awaiting dog.

Pat Rodwell

Raining Frogs

Joinings Bank - Langley Hall hidden by trees on the right

I lived in Langley Road, opposite "The Hall", which was the doctor's house. One afternoon during the war I was walking up Joining's Bank to meet my mother. It was raining and quite windy. Suddenly there was a whirlwind in the trees, sending the leaves swinging, then it started to pour down and tiny little dark green, almost black frogs fell from the trees. I ran to go back home, trying not to step on them, they poured down the gutters and into the drains. It was all over in a matter of minutes. It was said that they came from the jungles in the winds - an experience I will never forget. Arthur C Clarke confirmed this sighting later in his books.

Peggy Cowley

Chapter Six
The Post War Years

Titford Road School

Titford Road School - a class in 1946

I was born and brought up in Jarvis Crescent and the Titford canal was always part of my childhood. We spent our days playing by the canal, the lake, and a lot of the time on the tip, or the allotments. I always thought that we lived in the country. The canal in those days was more like a river bank, with the horse drawn barges an everyday occurrence, except when the water was frozen over, then the ice barge really was something exciting to run and look at.

I really can't remember much about my lessons at Titford Road School. I can remember doing games and gym in the playground dressed only in our knickers and vests, and having to run across the playground in all weathers to go to the toilet. Playtimes would be spent doing stickups (handstands) against the wall, or skipping. At home we played at spinning tops, skipping, marbles, hopscotch, cricket using the pigbin as wickets and french cricket - also a strange game where we raced up and down hitting a bicycle wheel with a stick.

Jennifer Cullwick (née Cox)

School Meals Service

Borough of Oldbury School Meals Service in the late 40s - regular visitors to Titford Road School

The "Black Hand Gang"

I went to Moat Farm Schools between 1942 and 1948 and was a member of the "Black Hand Gang". We were all from around the Brookfields Road area. We used to play "kick the can" and tie people's doorhandles together and go fishing in "The Springies" (now Defford Drive).

I remember my sister climbing right to the top of the gas lamppost - I wasn't brave enough. Just then we saw the point of the policeman's helmet coming down Reservoir Road.

We all scarpered and hid behind the privet, leaving my sister
up the lamppost.

"Coop" of the "Black Hand Gang"

Bonfires in the street

We used to have bonfires actually in the street and sit on the
gutter step eating jacket potatoes, faggots and peas, roast
chestnuts and the like. It was a proper street party, where all
the families in the street supplied something from their
rations. One year it was such a good bonfire that we burnt a
hole in the road!

Brenda McCrea

Milk deliveries

I remember milk being delivered by the Whitehouse sisters in
their pony and trap. Their farm was at the junction of Farm
Road and Pound Road. The milk was in churns on the back of
the trap with the measures hanging on a bar at the rear. I took
a jug to be filled with the required amount.

Brian Jones

A Mellor

Arthur Mellor, cobbler and clogmaker, had a shop in Trinity
Street next door to Watkins' first cycle shop. Arthur Mellor
purchased the very first bike sold by Watkins's - a "Raleigh
All Steel". They left Trinity Street and moved to High Street
before we did - we were one of the last shops left in the street,
when we finally moved.

Ray Watkins

F R Bastable & Son

My father, Reg Bastable, was born and bred in Langley and ran motor dismantling yards in Titford Road until 1948. He then left the area , but continued in the same trade.

After a brief retirement he decided to come back and open a car spares shop in Langley. We opened at 29 High Street in 1965. As the business expanded we bought more property and we are now based at 33.

Curly Bastable

Williams Garage, Langley Green Road

The Williams family owned the garage from the 1920s to the 1950s. *"Buy a bike you will never buy that bus"* was the slogan over the shop. They were the local agents for Royal Enfield cycles and Meccano and Hornby train sets.

In 1940 Fred Williams died and his son, Geoff, was called up for the Royal Air Force. Mrs Williams was left to run the garage on her own - at this time petrol was 11d per gallon. My family were very good friends with the Williams family and in my spare time I helped out by serving petrol and working in the shop.

Geoff returned after the war to carry on the business as before, but in 1950-1960 the garage was sold for development and he moved away.

P West

The "Coalmon"

I began working for Billy Slade the coal merchant early in January 1946. His yard was by the canal, on the Langley Green Road side of Uncle Ben's Bridge. There were usually four of us on the lorry doing house to house deliveries, and it didn't go down well at first - I'd just been demobbed, and whatever I'd been doing for the last few years, hard work didn't much figure in it. I think I managed to pull my weight, but with a struggle to begin with, I didn't get the sack anyway.

The customers had to be registered with us; they were rationed to five one-hundred-weight bags per household per month if my memory is correct, and I seem to remember that this was made up of two kinds of coal, best and second best, two of one and three of the other.

What this meant was that people were especially vigilant as to the quality as well as the quantity delivered. There's not much to be said for standing with a bag of coal on your back while the householder checks that all is well, but who could blame them. It did infuriate me when we had to stand there while someone cleared a space in the coal-shed and then afterwards grumbled that we'd made a mess - which it was difficult not to do.

I liked Billy Slade, I liked working for him, and in time, as the weather improved, I could have liked the work - but Bill's idea of getting another truck for me to work didn't materialise, there was a problem in getting the necessary permits for those things then, so all in all I didn't really see a future in it. But to slip across the other side of the counter for a while is an exercise that I can recommend - don't be a "coal-mon" though if you're in rooms with no proper bathing facilities!

Bill Hipkiss

David Slade & Sons
My grandfather William Henry Slade looked after the coal yards until his death in 1937, when they were taken over by his eldest son William - known as Bill.

William Henry Slade (1869-1937) had a sister Agnes, who married Fred Billington, a partner in Rood End Foundry. They were the parents of Fred Billington, the chemist. A lot of the Slade family lived in Old Park Lane - William Henry lived at 42 - and they had their own family pews in the Spring Street Chapel.

Derek Chambers (grandson of William Henry Slade)

A much earlier photograph showing the coal wharves & Langley Forge

The "Quick Service" bike shop

In 1938 our family business, which had started in 1933, moved to 336 Londonderry Road, where an electrical shop (Weldon's) had become available. It moved again, across the road, to number 269 in February of 1946.

Number 269 was built in 1934 as a hair dressing salon by a Mr Marshall. The salon closed at the outbreak of war and its goods were stored. It never reopened - until it became "Quick Service (Londonderry) Ltd". The property was used for various related businesses until it was sold for redevelopment in 1996 and the business moved south.

No. 269 Londonderry Road, the Quick Service Shop ca 1950

The main business was the sale, repair and building of bicycles and the sale of their spare parts and accessories, and mopeds, although the sale and servicing of electrical goods was also a main line.

Over the years other services were provided: accumulators (jars) for battery radios were charged up, a florist and garden supplies, bookings for Mann's Coaches of Smethwick were taken, a collection point for Smethwick

Laundry was operated and paraffin for stoves was sold and delivered.

John Hodgkins

No. 336 Londonderry Road . The Quick Service Shop taken ca 1950. Although it advertises the Smethwick Laundry, its address was Langley.

A E Watkins & Sons

We originally opened our shops at 19 and 21A Trinity Street, Langley on 25th February 1946. Cycles and electrical goods of the day were sold. With the arrival of television we developed into television sales and opened two more shops in Trinity Street - one as a service department and the other firstly as a record shop and then specialising in prams and baby equipment.

154

Mr Alfred Edward Watkins outside the first shop in Trinity Street

Watkins' first High Street premises - previously Moyle & Adams and Green & Kelly's on the site of the present car park

We then took over the premises in the High Street, originally Green & Kelly's, and lastly in 1951 we took over Moyle & Adams shop, which we made into a furniture department. These shops stood next to each other opposite the "Crosswells" Inn on the site of the present car park. We traded there until 1974, when we moved into our present purpose-built unit on the site of the Langley Institute, which was demolished in 1973.

Ray Watkins

The 1947 Winter

Moat Road in the snow 1947

That particular year, I was employed at M. Myers & Co., pens and stationer's sundries manufacturers, situated in Hall Street, Langley. Throughout that long, particularly bitter winter there

156

was an acute fuel shortage, especially of coal and coke. Many firms were then heated by coke-fed boilers, so emergency working conditions had to be put into effect. The working week was condensed into four 12-hour shifts. The firm closing down on Fridays and Mondays to save fuel.

At home we had very little coal; some people mixed coal dust with wet cement and packed it into plant pots to set into "brickettes to burn, or rather smoulder and spit, when they got hot. Bedrooms were not heated - I remember going to bed wearing cardigans, woolly hats and gloves to keep me warm!

Even though the war had been over for two years, most food was still rationed and for several years on we could only buy meat and grocery from the shops where we were officially registered.

Pat Rodwell

I remember walking up the Wolverhampton Road and the snow was higher than my shoulders. It had drifted eight to ten feet in parts.

Bill Hipkiss

I remember driving along the Wolverhampton Road in the big freeze of 1947 in my old Morris. The surface was so treacherous that some of the suspension springs fell out of my car as I was driving along! When workmen tried to clear the road the ice was so embedded that it took huge chunks of tarmac up with it.

Eric Fanthom

As Grafton Road was a "dead end" traffic other than delivery vehicles didn't use to come up further than Woodnorton Road and during the heavy winter of 1947 we were completely cut off. I recall we had to go to the bottom of Grafton Road to collect the milk and bread from the delivery vans and my brother took his sledge to fetch coal for us and other neighbours from the coal lorry parked by "The Barrel", because the lorry couldn't get through the snow.

Audrey Taylor

Made in Oldbury

In 1949 (30th March - 2nd April) "an exhibition of local industrial effort" entitled "Made in Oldbury" was held at the Langley Baths.

Mr K H Wilson, Chairman of the Oldbury Local Employment Committee says in the Souvenir Handbook (price 6d) "Much has been written and more said in public during recent months about production and the need for more and more of it if our country is to succeed in its fight for economic stability... A very large number of the main products of Oldbury works are not "finished articles"... They are largely raw materials for the fabrication or production of many goods seen in the shops or used by all of us every day".

The Mayor of Oldbury, Mr B T Robbins, pointed out that "the variety of production in the local works, and the consequent call for labour... has brought workers here from all parts of England, Scotland and Wales, and it is that demand, created by local industry, which has been chiefly responsible for (the Borough of) Oldbury's population rising by more than a thousand people a year over the past two decades. He also criticised the previous lack of planning: "We only have to look around the older parts of Langley and Oldbury to see what happens when factories are erected on any piece of land which happens to be handy... You have industry held up because it has developed in congested areas where factory expansion and road improvements are both ruled out by lack of space. You have people living in houses continually shaken by the fall of drop-hammers, or where cleanliness is impossible because of the smoke which ... inevitably emerges from the factory chimneys".

Among the numerous exhibitors at the exhibition were:

The Albion Bottle Company, Rood End Road
"One of Oldbury's newest industries, and probably its most highly mechanised ... with an output of over 50 million bottles a year".

Parkes Classic Confectionery Ltd, Crosswells Road
"Founded in 1904 by Mr Parkes, himself a Langley man....and his traditions are carried on by Mr J Statham, works manager. ...The works are the largest in their section of the confectionery trade in the Midlands".

M C L & Repetition Ltd, Pool Lane
"Since they came to Oldbury 25 years ago - before the Wolverhampton Road was cut - M C L have pioneered accurate repetition work to very fine limits ... Precision repetition work is their speciality, in any metal ... three-quarters of their products eventually find their way overseas as component parts of motor-cars, radios or other products of British industry".

Hughes Johnson Ltd

"To two foremen from Tangye's of Smethwick, Oldbury owes the founding of Hughes Johnson. James Hughes, a blacksmith, was one of the pioneers of drop forging, with his partner, Richard Johnson, who had been a fitter...While the firm was started in 1877, drop forging did not become part of their interests until a year or two later ...

"Early output was directed to forgings for agricultural machinery and marine work. Later came the bicycle and the automobile. Already having a reputation for high class work, the company was naturally called on to produce forgings for early aircraft, and drop forgings made at Langley were airborne in 1910...

"A subsidiary company, Light Metal Forgings Ltd, was formed to operate a forge devoted exclusively to light alloys. Much of the output from both firms still goes to the aircraft industry".

An early photograph of the Hughes Johnson work force

Imperial Chemical Industries Ltd

"At their Chance & Hunt Works, I.C.I's General Chemicals Division is making an all-out effort to keep up with the demands for sulphuric acid. That is always good news for Oldbury, because sulphuric acid is a trade "barometer" - when consumption is high, trade is booming, for it is an essential in so many industries from the pickling of steel plates to the manufacture of rayon, and from agricultural fertilisers to the accumulator and battery acid in which form most of us know it best.

"The Chance & Hunt Works - pioneers of Oldbury's great chemical industry of today - were founded in 1835".

British Industrial Plastics Ltd

"Shortly after the first world war, due to difficult trading conditions, the Company, then the British Cyanides Co.Ltd., found itself in desperately low water. One of the factories was closed down, a cut in pay was accepted all round and the research staff worked with redoubled energy to find a new product to restore prosperity. In 1926 "Beetle" moulding powder was evolved - the first white moulding powder in the world; soon the works were even busier than ever...

"Today, BIP products contribute to the manufacture of countless industrial components and household articles. All because a group of men, working in Oldbury, wouldn't give up ..."

taken from "Made in Oldbury Souvenir Handbook"

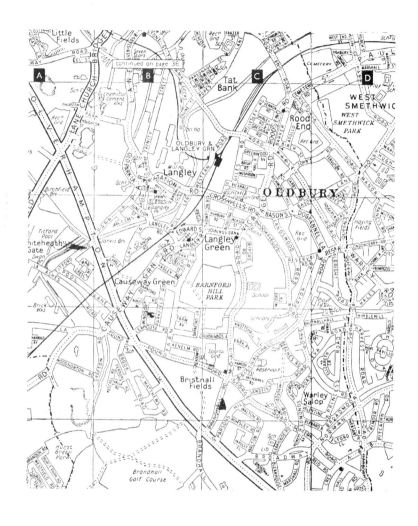

Langley area street map of the 1950s
Reproduced by kind permission of
the Geographers' A-Z Map Co Ltd.

Chapter Seven
The Fifties

Housing

The early 1950s were not easy for people starting out in married life. There was a post-war housing shortage. To get a council house in Langley and Oldbury meant a wait of around 10 years. Permits, needed before you could have a new house built, were difficult to obtain.

At the time rents were not controlled and were open to exploitation. Most newly-weds lived with parents or in-laws until a home of their own could be found. My husband's parents let us have two rooms in their home for the first five years of our married life.

Pat Rodwell

The end of the Second World War brought with it a need to provide housing for returning servicemen and those whose homes had been destroyed. The "Pre-Fab" was born. The "Pre-Fab" was a pre-fabricated, one storey unit house, produced in factories and then transported to sites.

There were two patterns: a smooth aluminium skin on a framework containing insulation, or concrete decorative panels with a rough-cast effect. Pre-Fabs, in their time, were leaders in comfort and convenience and although their stated life was 10 years, some are still lived in today.

The "Pre-Fabs" came at the same time as the restrictions on purchasing goods. Returning servicemen and newly-weds had "dockets" to buy utility furniture.

James Durrant

During the 1939/45 war, to economise on resources, a type of furniture was produced that was known as "Utility Furniture". Such furniture was quite plain but durable; we bought some in1943 and two pieces are still in use after 54 years.

Bill Hipkiss

Fragnoli's New Cart

Our father's first name was Giuseppe, but in the family he was called Joseph, the English equivalent. Locally people referred to him as "Ice cream Jack" or "Ice cream Billy".

Fragnoli's brand new ice cream cart, right up to the minute, with hot running water and washing facilities

Our father gained a number of diplomas for the purity and quality of his ice cream and was so proud that he advertised the fact on his new cart. Our sister Mary, shown in the photograph, carried on making the ice cream after his death in 1956. Mary and Annie continued with the shop and the ice cream making until 1976, when they retired.

Teresa Jaynes & Louisa Nash (née Fragnoli)

Apprentice Daze

To a brand new apprentice the Albright & Wilson site of the early 1950s was an enchanting wonderland of action, smells, powder and fire.

Opposite the door of the Test Room workshop was an intricate brick building, built on the wall of the Oxford. Scruffy from long use, full of low walls, wooden stairs and platforms. On these bubbled big vats. Occasionally a fascinated watcher from a doorway would hear a loud soft plop, and see an 18 inch tall candle-like flame shoot out of a vat, burn for a second and disappear. Nobody took any notice, the men worked safely.

Another doorway for a naive watcher was in the Amorphous Phosphorus Plant (the dark strip on the side of Bryant & May safety matches). This was Bottomside against Chances wall behind the Company Offices. It was a similar complicated brick building, like the other but bigger and it seemed older and much more well used. Here the watcher could see iron baths, maybe 12 inches wide, 24 tall, and 60 long, full of raw material pushed into ovens or being removed when "cooked". As they were pulled out onto the work floor the filling could be seen as red concrete. A process worker topped it up with a gallon or two of water before grabbing his pneumatic road breaking hammer and jumping up to stand on top. He had to break up the mass into pieces he could shovel out. The fun was to wait for the moment that the chisel made an air tunnel down to the point where it could strike the red phos. Then with a loud sploshy crack a waterspout of red liquid would head for the ceiling. Very entertaining, but the worker took no notice.

The main entrance to the Langley works was 200 yards down the Oxford. It was a huge pair of steel paling gates alongside a red brick office block (3 floors) with the commissionaires Lobby. Opposite was a similar entrance for Bottomside, except that the office block was older and better built. Inside it had lots of polished wood, carpets and tiled floors. It had a receptionist at the door and the Exchange for the works internal phone system in the basement (Mr G Jaynes domain). The offices were connected by a covered bridge and also a tunnel under the Oxford.

Either side of the Lobby were the machines for clocking in/out (about 300 workmen to each of 8 machines). The "clocks" were about the size of an upright piano. Each had side windows to see the recordings and a fixed wheel (30" dia.) at the end facing the Works, (the Fitting shop). The rim of the wheel was filled with a row of small holes each with a numbered label. One end of the hollow centre shaft was fixed to a drum carrying the time recording chart and the other to an arm reaching to the rim. The arm had levers and ended in a peg to go through a hole and a brass knob to locate the arm and push the peg. To clock (punch the clock), the arm was swung over "your" hole and the knob pushed until a ding signalled the time had been stamped.

Long files of men would form in front of each clock at finishing time. If the person in front was feeling irritable he would give the arm a good swing after clocking out. Bruised and bleeding fingers could result from trying to catch it (always use left hand). The few seconds this took were enough for cat calls of "hurry up" or more ribald ones about "finding the number" to ring out.

Soon after I first started the winter weather made me late. I pushed my bike through the Lobby but found a bolt in

166

my clock hole. Out it came, I clocked and went on to the cycle racks. A bellow came from behind me and a big stout commissionaire rushed out. (He seemed likely to grab my ear and run me off to the Headmaster!) My first brush with the Lates System.

If a workman was over 5 minutes late he was "pegged". The bolt would not be removed (and pay started) until acceptable explanations were made to the Commissionaire and then to the foreman. Over the week a total of 15 minutes late was allowed, after that men were sent home.

My foreman Mr Percy Ballard told me to join Old Billy Bastable on his Chart changing and meter reading rounds. These were Steam, Water towns and cooling, Gas, Electricity and other consumables. Costs of running many of the plants were then worked out by clerk Joe on a Fowler 144 inch drum sliderule calculator.

Old Bill seemed to know all the nooks and crannies of the Oldbury site and most of the process men. Going around with him was an education in itself. He could tell me what the plants did and for many their history since the war, WWI. He also told me war stories, WWI & WWII, and how to make a jigsaw puzzle from the paper wrapper of five Wills Woodbines. The meter rounds weren't all Bottomside/ Topside/HM Factory, one was off the site. We had to read the Bore hole water meters up Crosswells Road as far as the Merrivale: we always got back just in time for lunch.

I also accompanied Mr Ernie Jones (an old SW&S man) off site. Mr Albright had asked for repairs to the timer/controller of his domestic hot water system. We were to make them. It was my first chauffeur driven ride, out to his big posh house in the country. A nerve-wracking assignment.

167

Wipe feet and hands, very deferential, careful with furniture, tidy up properly, make very sure that the trouble was fixed.

Later the opposite, a visit to the Rattlechains water-filled marl hole. Waste was taken there by narrow boat (Clayton's) and water checks were made periodically.

Consumables and material for repairs were available with a Stores Note, from the stores by the main gate into Bottomside. One day I was sent there, to one armed Bill, with a note for "best paper" (we often withdrew old rags for cleaning equipment). He said "Out of stock. Go up the Oxford to the place on the corner". I started out, then it dawned - the place was Lloyd Bank. I went back to the workshop and asked for a PASS-OUT to go off Company property. Honours evened I thought.

A "Tap out" of a Phos. Furnace was spectacular. Tapered wooden billets about 4 ft. long had been rammed into the carbon-lined tap hole and capped with clay. this burnt solid. In the days before Oxyiron thermal lances, men spent hours with steel bars and sledge hammers clearing it, so that the tons of molten slag would run out and allow a new charge in. (Sometimes a furnace would self-tap, that sent men running to prepare the pits to receive it). The slag runs out via a huge steel cauldron (to catch the Ferro Phosphorus) and into a common pit floored with the remains of previous taps. Here, after being squirted with cooling water, caterpillar mounted, forward bucket rear trap door steel rope operated diggers would lift chunks into the T&S Elements lorries. These left via the Top Gate into Langley. Some residents may remember the slightly steaming loads going through Langley.

The works canteen (dinner & sweet 1s 10d or 9p) was near the end of the Oxford. Organisation was slick enough to allow time for a walk after lunch. Workmen and us apprentices would walk into Langley village - to window shop (maybe buy a record in one of Watkins shops) or on up to High Street to the Park for an informal football knockabout.

Another walk took us into the "green countryside". By turning right down Park Lane and then left up Old Park Lane, towards the Titford Road Schools, a path to the Birchley crossing bus garage could be reached. The path ran between the "Blue Billy" spoil heaps. Near Churchbridge it passed a huge pool maybe 300 yards in diameter. This black, smelly, evil-looking water was a disused marl hole, reputed to be bottomless and toxic. Robust weeds had colonised the whole area making a relief from bricks and mortar.

Many years later (1970) the pool was pumped empty to allow the M5 motorway to be built. This revealed almost vertical sides plunging down maybe 100ft to a flat bottom. The underwater surfaces had turned jet black, without a sign of greenery or weeds. Very horrible and smelly but to me the surprise was the remains of the old workings.

Near the centre of the floor of the hole was a tall brickwork tower. Mounted horizontally on top was a large (maybe 10 ft. dia.) wheel. In one side (SW) of the pit was an arch of brickwork (maybe 30 ft. tall) that seemed to be the entrance to a tunnel to an adjacent pit (for a ropeway?). Rightly judged a place to avoid, definitely not good for swimming or boating, it was still a very interesting piece of industrial archaeology. It was located almost as near to the middle of Langley village as the hole at the end of the Oxford (under Albright & Wilson's "New Lab"), which was presumably of very much the same size, date and utility.

by an Albright & Wilsonite

Rivalling New York

Langley's only "skyscraper" is situated in Thompson Road. It was opened in 1957 by the Mayor of Oldbury, and named after him, "Alfred Gunn House".

Processions & Celebrations

Festival of Britain 1951. Float outside Lloyds Bank & the Co-Op. Watkins' shop in the background.

During Coronation Week the Langley Prize Band and the Salvation Army Band gave concerts every evening in the local parks. The Borough of Oldbury provided souvenir gifts for many of its residents, the most generous being a savings account containing two guineas for each baby born on Coronation Day of Oldbury parents resident in the Borough.

taken from the Coronation Souvenir

Coronation float in Causeway Green Road 1953

Carnival procession at Langley Green

171

Langley Carnival Queen Jean Beckett (née Withers) in the first big carnival after the war 1953

Holy Trinity & St. Michael's Church choirs in Langley Park

172

Langley Ladies and Girls Choir

Langley Ladies & Girls Choir - the first concert

The minister Reverent Percy Myers held a dedication service for the choir, which was formed in the 1950s. The choir was disbanded when its conductor Beryl Taylor (centre in front row) died in 1979. The pianist, Rose Pullinger, can be seen to the right of Beryl. I am second from the right in the back row.

I can remember two of the costumes the choir had - one was a delicate green satin, the other a kingfisher blue taffeta. We went all over the place to sing - one of the most memorable was Winson Green Prison. I remember singing "The Happy Wanderer" and "We'll Gather Lilacs", as well as sacred music. One of the choir, Mrs Newby (third from the left in the back row), recited monologues and told funny stories and Black Country jokes - she always got a standing ovation.

Gwen Davies (née Stevens)

173

Barlow Homes

Mrs J U Barlow laying the foundation stone in 1954, with the Mayor, Alderman John Donald Beard

Official opening by Mayor, Alderman Alfred Gunn in 1957

Mr Charles Thomas Barlow OBE , a local industrialist who was mayor of Oldbury 1942-1945, together with his wife Mrs Jessie Barlow, donated nearly £50,000 to the people of Oldbury to provide either a maternity hospital or, as eventually happened, to provide low rent accommodation for elderly people. As well as bungalows and accommodation for wardens, a residents' social centre was built roughly where Whitehouse's Farm had originally stood.

information from the Official Opening Souvenir

Oldbury Grammar School

By the time I attended in the 50s, the open air corridors had long been enclosed, and the swimming pool was used only by frogs, while we went to Langley Baths down the road.

Control of the school (formerly known as the County High) had reverted to Oldbury Borough Council, and it had been renamed "Oldbury Grammar School". It was set to develop again after the difficulties of the war period.

Fortunately, straw boaters for boys were a thing of the past, but the school uniform was still distinctive, the blazer being green, blue and white vertical stripes. It was clear which school you went to, and there was no hiding place for a "grammar grub" of the fifties.

The school song had been written in 1926 by the headmaster, J G Howarth. It was a product of its age, and the words were not taken seriously by most of us who sang it thirty years later. I remember two lines of our rewritten version: instead of *"Though the strife of life may be swift and keen, though we may find hard knocks to rule..."*, we substituted those school colours *"Though the stripes of life may be dirty green, or white and faded blue...."*

We had to be careful not to let the headmaster hear, for Dr Howard would certainly not have approved! He was a commanding figure, upright in both attitude and stature - a headmaster of the old school with gown and, when necessary, cane. He conducted the school orchestra for many years, and I often wondered what his real reaction was to the dance band started by Mr Eacott.

Music was an important part of school life with various orchestras, groups and choirs. A Jubilee Appeal in 1954 and the Dawes Memorial Fund saw the installation of a fine pipe organ in the school hall. It was used at speech days and concerts, and our hymns at assembly were sung to its strains each morning.

Annual school plays were reintroduced in the late fifties under the direction of Harry Laycock. Somehow he persuaded me to play a Japanese poet in "The Nightingale", but I think he regretted it as rehearsals proceeded!

The cast of "The Nightingale", directed by Harry Laycock (centre) in 1959. This was the second post-war school play.

The school achieved high standards in many areas including sporting activities, and gained a reputation for "academic excellence", long before that phrase became part of all school statements!

The ex-pupils association, the "Cresconians" took their name from the school motto "Cresco" (I grow). They were active in Langley life for many years, running social events, an amateur dramatic society and sports clubs. The main society folded in the sixties, but the football club marked fifty years of competition with a dinner in 1971. I remember watching them play on many local pitches, often now built over, including Chance and Hunts Social Club in Dog Kennel Lane and Wootton's fields off Langley Road.

It ceased to be a grammar school on 31st August 1974, when secondary education was reorganised in the borough, and it became Langley High School, a non-selective secondary school.

Terry Daniels (pupil 1954-61)

Return of the Frogs

The Moat Farm was built over in the 1930s, but the pool and some boggy fields remained until 1953. The track across the pool dam became Matty Road. Springfield Road and Clee Road were built on the pool and Tudor Road on the boggy field above Langley Swimming Baths. The estate was occupied during the bad winter of 1953.

The following spring the frogs returned to spawn. Residents remember the frogs were everywhere. In places they were so thick on the ground that they had to be swept up.

Londonderry Lad

Causeway Green Primary School

The school was officially opened by Major M.F S Jewell on 27th March 1954. The Chairman at the event was the Mayor of Oldbury, Councillor F W Thompson.

It was the first new school to be completed in Oldbury since the end of the war and it was proposed that it would, in the future, "serve as the main contributory school to the proposed Whiteheath Secondary Modern".

The Infants' School, with accommodation for 240 children, was first occupied in September 1952. The Junior School had accomodation for 320. Headteachers were Miss W A Sendell (infants) and Mr R Morrison (junior).

from a newspaper article of the time

Hughes-Johnson Amateur Dramatic Society

I worked for Hughes-Johnson for over 25 years, mostly in the progress office. In the 1950s some of us on the staff formed an Amateur Dramatic Society and put on several plays in the Works Canteen. On dress rehearsal night we used to invite the pensioners of the area to come and watch the play and gave them tea and cakes in the interval. They often used to ask when the next play was on.

Vera Angus (née Hadley)

Oldbury Rep

This thriving theatre moved to its present site in Spring Street, Langley in 1956. The building, originally the Spring Street Methodist Chapel, has been thoroughly renovated. Oldbury Repertory Players was formed as an independent theatre company on 24th July.

Chapter Eight
The Sixties

Christmas at A Oakes, Rood End

Many local people remember the toy department when it was on the first floor of our store. Santa's grotto first appeared after the second world war, when someone from the Barlow Theatre came to help us with the artwork for the original grotto. In 1966 we were advertising a visit to Santa's grotto with a parcel from Santa for 2/-.

Robert Oakes

A&W Pensioner Harry Mills and the Famous "Village" Clock

The clock with its four faces, atop the old Albright & Wilson Office Block in Trinity Street was a very well known landmark. The "Oxford", the local name for Trinity Street, was a busy thoroughfare in the first half of this century. Every day hundreds of passers-by would set their watches by the reliable old "Village" clock or speed up on their way to work.

Harry Mills, A & W pensioner, worked for the company from 1960-1990. One of his jobs in the early days was to wind the clock every eight days. The key was a mighty affair that took two hands and a test of strength by Harry just to turn it. In about 1975 the mechanical drive was replaced by an electrical one.

During his days as "Master of the Clock", Harry once found a note attached to the movement indicating that it was

179

then 97 years old. That was over 12 years ago, so Harry reckons the clock is over 109 years old.

Tom Tomlinson

Harry Mills & the Clock

Holy Trinity

By the time the last christening took place in 1959 and the final wedding in 1960, the church was blackened by pollution and in a bad state of repair, unrecognisable as the once beautiful building it had been.

Holy Trinity was officially closed in 1960 but stood empty and at the mercy of vandals a further eight years.

Tucked away on the back page of the "Warley News Telephone" of 19 September 1968 is a brief article about the demolition, with a photograph showing the gutted interior.

After the demolition was complete the site was levelled, grassed over and planted with rose-beds. Despite its name of Trinity Green it has appeared to visitors as no more than a traffic island since that time and nothing marks it as a place of burial.

Verna Gibbons

On the Passing of Holy Trinity, Langley

If you're near Langley centre, with all of its change,
    there's a sad little feature, an island of green;
not so long ago sat there a small, fusty church,
    and those sentinel trees harbour graves in between.

If you pause for a while, and above all the noise
    of the worldly encroachments that ply round this place,
you might hear a choir sing - and if I should be near
    you might just spot a tear sneak away down my face.

That's because I'll be matching each voice to a name,
    and each name to a face - to a laugh or a smile;
and you know, I'll be sighing a sigh of regret
    that the blending of voices was just for a while:

and the resolute blending of minds and of means
    was too late but to make pure remorsefulness vain;
we forsook her with eagerness, brimful of lust -
    and no more, for our blood, will her bell ring again.

181

Yet perhaps at the end of our sad, little day
we might hear the tolls urge as they never did then;
or a discarnate choir, just a pulse-beat away,
and join in at the end with a long, low "Amen". . .

Bill Hipkiss

St John's - a new parish

A mission church under Christchurch Oldbury served the Tat Bank area, meeting first in Tat Bank Infants School and later in the Church of St John the Evangelist in Tat Bank Road. This was built in 1897 at a cost of £1,400 on land given by Messrs Chance. The church relocated to a new building in St Johns Road, Rood End in 1915.

In 1969 St John's became the parish church of a second Langley Parish, formed by taking over an area covered by Oldbury Parish Church.

from Church records

Dyson's Mission

Warley News Telephone of 30 November 1967 ran an article describing the loss of the Mission Hall as tragic. The Mission was on land sold to Hughes Johnson Stamping Co. Ltd by British Rail without the knowledge of the Mission trustees, who were given notice to quit by Christmas Day 1967.

John Horner, M.P. for Oldbury and Halesowen, appealed direct to Hughes Johnson to allow the Mission to remain. He commented that "This Mission is nothing to look at from the outside, but you can't judge things from what you see on the outside. I am making a bid to save a centre of friendliness, warmth, service and worship".

182

The Secretary, Mrs Phoebe Harley, said that the regular weekly attendance of about a hundred were all terribly disappointed about having to quit "We cannot understand why British Rail did not give us first refusal. We would have raised the money".

from "Warley News Telephone" 30 November 1967

"Adieu, Blue Billy"

In the 50s I used to go with my father to Mrs Beddows' shop in Park Lane to get our sweets for the week. Behind her shop and the houses lurked "Blue Billy"! Blue Billy was a chemical mound to the west of Park Lane, Langley, the result of dumping the by-products from the manufacture of sulphuric acid at Chance & Hunt. At least five generations of Langley inhabitants lived with it until it was finally removed and used to fill in the marl holes on the opposite side of Birchfield Lane and Churchbridge when the motorway was cut through in the 60s.

It was notorious enough to receive an editorial in "Chemistry and Industry" (11th October 1969) under the heading "Adieu, Blue Billy". It records the difficulties experienced in removing it and also in living with it for over a century!

"... the contractors met with "A giant bluish mound of chemical waste." Local press reports told of a labour force "stricken with strange maladies" and of workmen ... suffering from "an itching dust and a smell causing nausea". The issuing of breathing apparatus to the men, the installing of air filters in the local telephone exchange, and the hurried analysis of Blue Billy earth - all were reported as essential in the last battle against Oldbury alkali waste.

183

"Such agitations ... are like echoes of the many protests made during a century or more of activities by the historic Chance organisation. ... There were persistent demands for compensation, with property owners in the town suffering damage by the effluents and fumes ... We hear of "corroding gasses" blighting vegetation, of housewives with the incessant labour" involved in cleaning stained kitchen fittings ... parson Bowlby successfully claimed damages for the corrosion of his vicarage walls, while John Powell, the draper, claimed damages to his stock" (back in the 1850s and 60s!)

Our forefathers dumped the waste to make the mound, lived their lives next to it and probably played on it too - all before health, safety and the environment became concerns. Older members of my family recall in the 20s leaving St Michael's School at lunchtime, "taking father's dinner down to Chances", and being hardly able to see the way ahead down "the Oxford" because of the fumes and smoke. Others say you could ride a shiny bike into the Oxford and come out the other end on a dull one!

The chemical industry may have brought employment and prosperity to the area, but it was not a good neighbour in those days, and Blue Billy was typical of its effects.

Terry Daniels

The "Blue Billy"

It was a mound, or "bonk" to us locals, and it was opposite the Good Shepherd School in Churchbridge. Its purpose was to provide a dumping ground for the waste products from the chemical production at the Chance and Hunt Works in Park Lane, Oldbury.

As a boy I used to go up there often, it was ideal for tobogganing in the snow. During the second World War there were pill-boxes up there, and a huge map of England traced in the sand - all for the use of the Home Guard in the event of an invasion, a real threat. At the bottom, on what was known as "Sawyer's Field", trenches were dug, and near them, on the pavement, were placed drums of waste oil or paraffin every so many yards in order to create a thick, black smoke-screen when air-raids were on.

An industrial site now occupies the spot because the whole of the mound was moved in the late 50s and early 60s. In order to do this a bridge was constructed from the top of the "Billy", across Churchbridge, the road that leads into Oldbury, and ended at the twin marlholes in the apex formed by Portway Road and the Wolverhampton Road, a distance of perhaps a quarter of a mile or so. This soil was then used to fill the marlholes, but leaving a depression into which was landscaped a power sub-station.

George A Webb

The Coming of the Motorway

With the sixties came all the upheaval of the building of the motorway. The new M5 sliced through the area, largely on elevated sections, creating wastelands underneath and revolutionising transport in the region.

Considerable difficulties were experienced in constructing the elevated section over Titford Pool, which was at that time reputed to be bottomless.

M5 interchange area, showing construction of viaduct, with motortruck showroom on the Wolverhampton Road October 1967

Titford Branch Canal. Piling during the building of the M5 November 1967

Chapter Nine
The Seventies & Eighties

In his book "The Story of 100 Years of Phosphorus Making 1851 -1951" R E Threlfall mentions that, during the Second World War, the traitor William Joyce ("Lord Haw Haw") broadcasting from Berlin said "Albright & Wilson you can pull down your big chimney (it was demolished in 1941), but we can still find you". Lord Haw Haw was bluffing. The Luftwaffe never did find Albright & Wilson's and consequently Langley suffered little or no damage from air raids. In nearby Birmingham whole areas of houses, shops, factories and commercial premises were destroyed, so that after the war it was necessary to have a complete new building programme from the ground up. Langley was different.

Anyone looking at a street plan of Langley Village at the turn of the century and comparing it with a plan of the area in the 1960s would see little difference. Records show that a number of families were still running businesses from the same premises that their parents or grandparents had traded from at the turn of the century, although in some cases the nature of the business had changed. The same rows of terraced houses still existed, many of them back-to-back, some one-up-one-down and, even twenty years after the end of the Second World War, many of the houses still had no indoor sanitation and only the most basic of amenities.

In the late 60s and early 70s plans to redevelop Langley were drawn up by the then Warley County Borough Council. A number of public meetings and exhibitions were held to explain the proposals and show how the area would look after redevelopment.

Langley Green houses in the redevelopment area

The meetings were often quite lively and there was a great deal of opposition to the proposals. Many of the people who attended the meetings had lived in the same house all their lives and in some cases were the second or third generation of the family to have done so. People were reluctant to move away from friends and familiar surroundings, and made their feelings forcibly and eloquently known. As one elderly lady put it at one of the meetings:

"It's not just a matter of bricks and mortar, you can replace those, but you can't replace the feeling of belonging that comes with having lived in the same place all your life. Our homes for us contain memories of a lifetime, of both the good and the bad - of the happy times and the sad times. As you reach my age the place where you've spent your whole life seems at times to be haunted by the ghosts of the past - of the people you've known and happenings - and though you can move us to places with all mod cons, it'll never be the same again, because the ghosts will never find out where we've moved to, and if they do, I don't think they will bother to come and visit us".

An assurance was given to those people who said that they wanted to move back to Langley after the redevelopment was completed, that they could do so. This assurance however was greeted with a great deal of scepticism - scepticism that was eventually proved well founded.

Despite the opposition the clearance went ahead and about three hundred shops, houses and small factories fell victim to the bulldozer. The community was split up, and people were rehoused, many in multi-storey flats on the new estates that had been built in the 50s. Rebuilding started and, when the first phase was completed in the late 1970s, 101 new homes had been built, 64 of which were one bedroom flats for the elderly.

With fewer people living in Langley there was less demand for shops and the remaining shops also faced fierce competition from new supermarkets outside Langley.

However, despite the tribulations of the 70s and 80s, the upset caused by the redevelopment, unemployment caused by the closure of such places as Langley Forge, MCL, Parkes' Confectionery etc (many of whose employees lived in the Langley area), Langley survived. More council homes were built in Arden Grove and at New Henry Street and Edward Street, Langley Green. A new private housing development at what is now Westmead Drive and various small housing infills brought people back to the area.

John Sullivan

Parkes' Confectionery in Crosswells Road, now the Hot Shots Snooker Club

Langley folk, showing they still knew how to enjoy themselves, at a celebration to mark the Queen's Silver Jubilee in 1977

Causeway Green looking down towards Ashes Rd on the right 1970s

High Street looking towards Uncle Ben's Bridge, with the Langley Post Office (formerly the "Fountain" Inn) 1970

Langley Carnival revived

I revived the Langley carnival, which had been discontinued. I arranged the first in 1973, and it was all put together in six weeks. We had a procession led by a pipe band and World War II vehicles. We also staged the first outing of Bill Hunt's newly reconditioned "Leander" steam organ.

Lawrence Banner

191

Whyley Street with Spring Street on the right 1970

The Five Ways at Langley, from the High Street, showing the Co-op & the "Crosswells" Inn (which is the only building on the picture still standing) 1970

The Cancer Research Campaign

Since 1974 I have worked for the Cancer Research Campaign. I was "conned" into joining by my dear wife and it has been a very rewarding experience. I am proud as a "brummie" to be accepted by the people of Langley as a "local"!

Lawrence Banner

Edward Street Methodist Church in the 1980s

Edward Street Methodist Church, showing the demolition area, where houses now stand.

Mr Reg Payne, who successfully led the campaign to stop the church being closed, surveys the chaos while refurbishment is carried out in 1985

All of Edward Street was demolished apart from the church, which was saved because of a determined campaign led by Reg Payne. The majority of the people eventually moved down closer to Langley. There was talk that it was because the new motorway was going to come through Edward Street, although that never happened. Later the new Sunday School was built to replace the two 1914-1918 army huts, which had been the home of the old Sunday School.

Gwen Davies (née Stevens)

A widely known Langley figure

"Name's Harold", said the weather beaten man. A man of few words. Bareheaded, thick spectacles, dressed in a long grey coverall and wellies, a very familiar figure throughout the Langley area. He'd just brought his delivery bicycle in for a minor repair. He would be back in 15 or 20 minutes. The bike, fitted with big carriers front and rear, was his essential tool and constant companion.

For Harold was a "Paperboy" and had been for about fifty years.

We had serviced his bicycle many times between the war and 1975. In bad weather he donned an oil-skin and an army-style ear cap and carried on, always in wellingtons. Rarely riding the bike.

From his mother's newsagent shop in Station Road, in the block of houses and shops between the corner of Mill Lane and the level crossings, his rounds covered a vast area. They were so big that he could be seen finishing the delivery of morning papers in late afternoon. It was said that he made deliveries throughout the region between Low Town & Perry Hill and Rood End & Causeway Green.

When Mrs Harold died he continued deliveries for about 7 to 8 years, but the shop almost closed down. In about 1976, I believe, Harold died unexpectedly. They broke into the house when he missed a delivery. It was found that he had lived very frugally, being more concerned about maintaining deliveries than the house, shop or money.

Langley became a little blander when Harold stopped his round.

As told to John Hodgkins

Norman Tarplee - memories of A Langley Mon

I first met Norman Tarplee, when a Compulsory Purchase Order was placed on the houses in Old Park Lane, Langley. Norman came to one of my "Councillor's Advice Surgeries" and told me just what he thought about the proposal to move him out of his house and pull it down. He was a blunt spoken, articulate man, and when one had a conversation with Norman, one was left in no doubt about his views.

Despite his and other residents' opposition the clearance went ahead. The people were rehoused, the houses pulled down and the close-knit community that had been Old Park Lane split up. Norman moved to a sheltered housing scheme at St. Michael's Court, Causeway Green Road, Langley. He had a brand new flat with all "mod cons", but I can't believe he was ever as happy there as he had been in his little terraced house in Old Park Lane.

I continued to see Norman after he had moved and became aware of his vast knowledge about Langley and its' people. He could remember the people who lived in Old Park

Lane when he was a boy. Who-had-married-who, who-worked-where, what business a particular family or person was in. He would recite their names as if they were the Tribes of Israel. Starting at the bottom on one side of the Lane, go to the top and come down the other side; naming the whole families. Mothers, fathers, sons, daughters, sisters and brothers, sometimes four generations of the one family living in the same house.

Norman was born in 1916, and he always made it clear that although he was not born in Langley (he came to live in Old Park Lane when he was two weeks old), he regarded himself as a "Langley Mon". He had a lovely phrase to describe local people - to Norman they were "Langgarians", and anyone who came say from the other side of the Wolverhampton Road was not as Norman would put it a "True Langgarian". I think if Norman had had his way anyone who was not a "Langgarian" would have had to have a passport to shop in the High Street.

Norman had a fund of stories about Langley (too many to relate here), but my favourite is about a Julie Banner, who used to sharpen the carving knife on the front door step before carving the Sunday Joint. Norman said "Us kids used to sit on the wall opposite her house, and wait for Julie to come out, and while she was sharpening the knife she'd sing "We've got more mate than yow. We've got more mate than yow. We've got more mate than yow". Chuckling at the memory, he would add in his broad Black Country accent "Er used to loff er eye out".

Sadly Norman died in 1994. However in 1988 he recorded his memories on tape. For a flavour of life in Langley between the wars it is well worth listening to.

John Sullivan

196

The National Boat Rally 1978

When I was eight years old my family took up residence in Langley. The year was 1958. Even at that age, my understanding of the Black Country was that you were never far from canals.

My own local stretch of canal was then almost a dead arm of the BCN, terminating in the Titford Pool. This Langley stretch of canal starts at the Crow Lock - six locks to raise the water up to the level of Titford Pool itself.

To the average person this pool appears to have no purpose, but it has, in the past, played an important part in the greater scheme of things. The pool played a major part in the modernisation of this waterway. The rainfall from the Rowley Hills fed a volume of water into the pool, so carrying water through a culvert to feed the Rotten Park Reservoir at Edgbaston, Birmingham. This was indeed forward planning.

In earlier times Titford Pool served the needs of local pits in the hills - indeed there existed a network of narrow "tram lines" to move goods. The extent of this activity hastened the arrival of a steam powered beam engine, sited at the Crow Locks, to pump water back up the line in order to serve the needs of both the boats and the Edgbaston reservoir. Hence, close to the beam engine, "Engine" Street came into being.

In 1978 the Inland Waterways Association, formed to safeguard the interests of private boat owners, began a series of campaigns and rescue schemes, their goal being to preserve the "motorways of the canals" for all people for all time.

The 1978 Rally proved a major success. My own boat was one of over 200 gaily painted narrow boats. The rally left the people of Langley with the satisfying feeling that their country was truly a giant of industry due to the dedicated canal builders of long ago.

Ian Max Durrant

Boat Rally 1978 at Titford Pool

This event was a wonderful boost for British Waterways, boat owners, the Inland Waterways Association, the people of Langley and local businesses.

Imagine a really huge, secluded pool, surrounded by paths and towering hedges, a quiet haven for wildlife, approached from Langley by a single arm of a little used canal. This canal, on its way through Langley, passes factories, then under Uncle Ben's Bridge, past the old Canal House, past the Navigation Inn and under the road bridge (carrying the ever-moving heavy Birmingham to Wolverhampton traffic) in its last length before entering the pool.

As the date of the rally nears, single boats slowly appear, moving quietly into the area of the pool and its approaches. Then the invasion becomes more obvious until, come the rally weekend, the pool and the canal are totally occupied by assorted boats.

To the onlooker it may appear a disorganised arrangement, but this is far from the truth. All the boats have been told where they may berth within the pool - an ordered exercise to ensure safety and maximum numbers. Within the pool all boats are berthed "bow to centre", making a neat pattern around the whole pool. The rally commodore's boat takes centre place. At the height of the rally the narrow boats reach far back beyond Langley High Street, in a seemingly endless line.

The weather that bank holiday was very unkind, heavy showers of rain did nothing for walking traffic along the only tow path, but there was still good support from Langley folk. Stalls and exhibition stands covered the sides of the path surrounding the pool area adding further interest.

This rally was a huge success, culminating on Sunday morning with a visit from the Bishop of Birmingham, who conducted a Christian service from the Commodore's boat.

Langley folk showed their usual hospitality and the rally was a talking point for months to come.

James A Durrant

Looking down from the Merrivale traffic island towards the Baths & Joinings Bank

A tantalising glimpse under the railway bridge in Langley Green Road towards the Langley Green shopping area

Banner's Newsagent's

The new council-built shop in Langley High Street had stood empty for over 18 months and the resident newsagent in Trinity Street, Mr Coley, decided to retire, which left Langley without a newsagent's. I already had a shop on the Wolverhampton Road by the "New Navigation", next to Hubball the barbers, so I decided to take one of the new shops and opened a newsagent's. I was given the keys to the empty shell on 1st December and opened on 29th December 1975.

After five years it was burnt out overnight. The shop was only closed for three weeks. Meanwhile I ran the newsagent's from the chemist's next door. The business was sold in 1995.

Laurence Banner

Chapter Ten
The Nineties

The Albright Bombshell - July 1990

It had been a busy afternoon in the main offices of Albright & Wilson Oldbury Works that particular day in July 1990. Employees were looking forward to going home for the weekend - the weather was perfect - the garden beckoned. Then came the bombshell. Literally!

Workmen unearthed a massive 500lb wartime bomb while laying a new car park at the office block in Station Road. Very quickly the whole site was closed. Offices and laboratories were evacuated as army bomb disposal officers raced in from Hereford to deal with the monster.

More than a hundred people, many of them pensioners, were evacuated from their homes. A true wartime spirit prevailed, as the local residents found themselves at the Causeway Green Centre being fed sandwiches and hot tea. Dozens of firemen and ambulance crews stood by as police sealed off the area. There were real fears of a massive explosion.

The four-hour alert was called off after the army experts found the device to be an empty shell. It had been defused around fifty years ago and the case buried in the field. So the whole incident ended peacefully, but with just one element of irony. Since the bomb scare in 1990, it has been suggested that the device was not a 500lb high explosive bomb, but a phosphorus bomb. Many such bombs were dropped by the Germans, it seems that this one failed to detonate.

Detective Chief Inspector John Fisher of West Midlands Police said "In wartime bomb disposal staff were so busy that they simply only had time to make each device safe before moving to the next one".

It seems that the defused bomb, which probably came down some distance from the Works, was moved to the Albright & Wilson Factory, where the phosphorus was melted out.

The German phosphorus was put into stock to help with the British war effort. It turned out to be one consignment of phosphorus from Germany which they never did invoice us for!

Tom Tomlinson

The Clock with no nine, but two elevens

Set high in the wall of one of the maintenance shops within Albright & Wilson Oldbury Works, is a clock that has remained a mystery for as long as anyone can remember. The clock has two elevens in Roman numerals, but no nine!

It seems the clock left the original maker with the "funny numbers" set in place and it has been like it ever since.

The building which houses the clock is known as the Carbon Shop. Until recent years, huge blocks of carbon (graphite) were machined, shaped and fabricated into most intricate equipment used in the manufacture of phosphoric acid. Technology has changed and very little carbon work is required these days. However the skills of the craftsmen who worked the carbon are still preserved as is the clock with the two "elevens".

Tom Tomlinson

The clock in the wall of the Carbon Shop

Phosphorus retorts - recycling in Victorian times

In the early days of phosphorus making the raw materials were bones and crushed coal. The process was carried out in fire-clay retorts. Each retort was about 48 inches long by 8 inches internal diameter, the mouths being narrowed to about 3 inches inside. These retorts were made in their thousands on site. Great skill was required in the preparation of the clay, the forming of the bodies and the drying and firing.

Syrupy phosphoric acid, obtained from the bones was mixed with about one fourth of its weight of ground coal and dried to a black powder. This was packed into fire-clay retorts and set into direct coal fired furnaces. Phosphorus vapour was produced, condensed and collected for processing into a range of very useful products.

The retorts had a limited life. Used retorts were carted away and in many cases found a second life. They were used for building walls and making good the banks of streams. Many a back yard pigsty or hen house was built from them.

Fire-clay retorts were being replaced by electric furnaces in 1893. In 1895 the last retort had been emptied and the coal fired furnace put out. Retorts were no longer needed for phosphorus making - but their secondary applications lived on!

Tom Tomlinson

This wall in Shidas Lane is made up of recycled phosphorus retorts

Albright & Wilson Oldbury Works Today
Albright & Wilson Oldbury Works, which was founded in 1850 by Arthur Albright, continues to flourish in 1997.

"In 1850 we moved" Arthur wrote, "the bantling phosphorus and her twin sister, chlorate of potash, from Wheeleys Lane to Oldbury". The original two acre site was purchased from Chance Brothers for £1,182!

As demand for match chemicals grew so did the Works - rapid acquisition of adjoining land quickly brought the Works up to its current 60 acres. From the "bantling phosphorus Works", Albright & Wilson grew into a major international company and Oldbury Works still remains at the heart of it.

Albright & Wilson has manufacturing sites in Europe, America and Asia, sales in excess of £850 million and assets of £350 million. Oldbury Works houses the A & W International Technical Centre. Here over 100 top scientists, recruited world-wide, spearhead the research and development effort.

In total, the Works employs 650 people. On some twenty separate production plants, over 100,000 tons of various chemicals are produced each year. Flame retardants, water treatment chemicals, pharmaceutical intermediates, herbicides, a range of food products, toothpaste polishing agents, calcium food supplements, paint pigments, detergents, oil field chemicals, metal plating, pet foods and hard surface cleaners are just some of the applications for Oldbury products.

Oldbury Works now has some of the most advanced and the safest chemical processing plant in the world. Products from Oldbury are exported across the globe. In 1997 safety and protection of the environment are watch words. That commitment is ever present at Oldbury Works to carry it forward into the 21st century.

Tom Tomlinson

BIP at Oldbury Today

BIP employs 570 people on its Oldbury site, resulting in £12.5 million per year being put back into the community in the form of salaries and local rates. In addition we spend £2 million per year on capital projects with local contractors.

There are 6 autonomous businesses on our 27 acre site, producing speciality resins and plastic moulding materials. The company has agents and distributors worldwide.

In October 1995 the company was purchased from T & N plc by an investment team led by Advent International, one of the world's leading private equity capital organisations. With support from Advent International, BIP is once again developing as an independent company, with the freedom to grow in the ways most appropriate to its markets.

Visitors to the Oldbury site are unanimous in their commendation for our efforts to improve safety and impact on the environment. A significant amount of monitoring is carried out in our analytical and environmental monitoring laboratory. This testing, covering both air and water, ensures that we are in control of all releases from our processes. The Titford canal runs through the site with a number of geese returning annually to breed; we currently have 60 geese using the canal and the site in general as a breeding ground.

An important factor in being a good neighbour is our developing association with local schools and colleges. In particular we have an employee on the board of governors of Causeway Green Primary School and, in direct liaison with Warley High School (with whom we have just won a "Quality in Partnership Award"), BIP introduces students to the many different aspects of industry and commercial life.

Sylvia Milner

Moose in Langley

Langley has been the home of the local lodge (or club) of Moose International since the first meeting held at the canteen of Albright & Wilson on 5th December 1929.

Formally known as The Loyal Order of Moose, this Lodge, which is Oldbury-Langley Lodge number 95, is part of the largest service organisation in the world.

During its sixty eight years of continuous existence, the Lodge has met at various locations in Oldbury and for the last twelve years has met at the place of its birth namely Albright & Wilson Recreation Club in Station Road, Langley.

During this time, the Lodge has raised many thousands of pounds for local and national charities as well as fulfilling its original obligations to care for the widows and orphans of its members. The Welfare State having restricted the monetary side of this obligation has given the fraternity freedom to cover a wider need whilst making sure those we are primarily responsible for are in no way neglected.

The Loyal Order of Moose was originally a semi-secretive but not secret order with a ritualistic way of meeting, but it has not been afraid to move with the times and the members now meet in a modern club-like style with guest speakers to lively meetings enjoyed by members, guests and visitors from the several other local lodges. As well as the monthly meetings, a programme of social events widens the appeal to members.

The values of friendship and service to others which built the order in this country are as relevant today as they were in the hard twenties.

Alan Watkins (Secretary)

Memories of Barnford Hill Park

Who remembers Barnford as it used to be?
In its former glory there for all to see.
The putting green, the tennis courts and the Sons of Rest,
Of all the parks in Oldbury it surely was the best.

Who remembers Barnford and its lovely flower beds?
Well designed and planted in blues and pinks and reds,
Geraniums and fuchsias all adding to the scene,
Rose beds full of fragrant blooms by the bowling green.

Who remembers Barnford and its big green wooden shelter?
A haven when the winds did blow and rain began to pelter.
The office was at one end, the other end the shop,
And the bell that clanged at closing time was housed upon the top.

Who remembers Barnford and its garden for the blind?
Full of perfumed flowers, some of ever kind.
Roses over pergolas, a eucalyptus tree,
Giving welcome pleasure to those who could not see.

Who remembers Barnford and its rocky hill?
The views from there were marvellous, you can see them still.
We'd climb up to the very top and think it was a mountain,
Then run down past the sandpit for a drink from the fountain.

Who remembers Barnford in the summer time?
We'd lovely grass to play on and many a tree to climb.
We'd play along the war-path or the monkey-run.
Many hours we spent up there, didn't we have fun.

Who remembers Barnford as a magic place to be?
Sometimes we'd take a sandwich, a cake and a bottle of tea.
We'd have a game of rounders, French cricket, tennis too.
We were never bored in those days, there seemed so much to do.

Who remembers Barnford in the winter snow?
Sledging down its covered slopes, faces all aglow.
Snowball fights and Jack Frost biting toes and fingers,
Crying to Mom with chilblains, how the memory lingers.

Who remembers Barnford at the time of war?
They took away its railings to help make guns galore,
And planted up a cornfield and a Victory garden too,
To help to feed the nation, the likes of me and you.

Who remembers Barnford at the time of its decline?
When vandals came and wrecked it, this park of yours and mine
Graffiti on the shelter, football on the "green",
Cars parked on the tennis courts. Oh how sad the scene!

I know it has its friends now all working to protect it,
For future generations we hope will all respect it.
But in its former glory it will stay in my memory,
For I remember Barnford as it used to be.

Barbara Powell

The Friends of Barnford Park

In 1994, after two public meetings, a Park Users' Committee was set up under the chairmanship of Mr Charlie Chester with help from council officers and local councillors. In 1996 after another public meeting a second committee, The Friends of Barnford Park was set up, chaired by Dr John Lloyd. With the invaluable aid and guidance of solicitor Mr Ian Evitts a constitution was accepted by the Charity Commission in September 1997. The charity, "Friends of Barnford Park", is dedicated to raise funds for the restoration of the park and for the enjoyment of all the people of Langley.

Joyce Lloyd

An Ode to Langley

As you drive from Savacentre
On your way to Toys-R Us,
You'll see a sign for Langley,
And that, my friend, is us.

They reckon we're part of Oldbury,
Which may well be the case,
But Langley's got its own character,
We think it's a marvellous place.

It's the home of the Barlow Playhouse,
The only live theatre in town!
And we have a Prize Winning Band
Of countrywide renown.

There's lots of room for parking,
You can park all day for free,
Pubs and a Cafe and Chip Shop
So why not stop for tea?

You can buy a trombone in Langley,
Or some spark plugs to service your car,
Get your suit dry-cleaned for the wedding
And a hair-do so you look Lah-Di-Dah!

There's a Card Shop, a Baker, a Butcher,
A Cobbler, (the old fashioned kind)
A Fruit & Veg and a Florist,
And a Balti if cooking's a bind.

There's a Furniture Store with tellys
And fridges and lots. lots more,
An Outfitters to make you look "dapper",
And a Hardware and Fancy Goods Store.

Yes Langley boasts of a High Street
Full of shops, but no big names in sight,
So if you're looking for something different
Just take the left turn at the lights!

Mike Jones

Langley Traders Association

We formed in May 1990 to enquire after and discuss the redevelopment of the High Street with the Black Country Development Corporation and with Sandwell Metropolitan Borough Council.

We also negotiated with West Midlands Transport regarding a bus route along the High Street and held discussions with the police with regard to security in the locality.

The recent renovation and development of the Langley Park house was initiated by us.

Fundraising events throughout the year provide the Christmas lighting programme for the entertainment of local people.

Ray Watkins

Zion United Reformed Church, Langley Green

The photograph of the people of Zion United Reformed Church, Langley Green shows that they are a group of ordinary local people of all ages. Somewhere at the back is the most recent member - Richard Landon, the minister who was "inducted" on 6th September 1997.

People and minister together form the church - believers in Jesus Christ as their Saviour and Lord, who meet on Sundays and during the week. They learn from the Bible about being Christians for themselves and for others. They worship God in a way that seeks to combine traditional and contemporary material, and is not too formal. They share the Lord's Supper, and baptise the children of committed Christian parents, and older believers who have not been baptised. They pray for God's work and the needs of the community and wider world. They support and encourage each other in the various circumstances of their lives. They meet together for social events.

Minister and people believe that the Good News of Jesus Christ is vitally relevant today, and would like to tell others about it, especially since it is not so well understood now as it was. They hope they can do so in a gentle way, and show God's love to everyone at the same time. They are glad to be part of the community of Langley Green for the future as for the past.

Richard Landon

The Ebenezer Wesleyan Reform Church

Although a relative newcomer, the Ebenezer Wesleyan Reform Church is very much at the heart of Langley. Parent and toddler groups and a youth club meet regularly and the church is closely involved with the Christmas Lights celebrations. The Rev. Robert Brindley is the church's first full time minister since the mid 50s.

The original church was built in Hunt Street, Oldbury in 1873. With the redevelopment of Oldbury, this church was demolished and the site for a new church was found in Langley. During Langley's own redevelopment programme houses on the corner of Spring Street and High Street were demolished and the new church was built on this site in 1981. The new church incorporates the foundation stone of the old church and also preserves four of the original stained glass windows, which hang, framed and illuminated, on either side of a cross made from timbers salvaged from the pews of the old church.

Barrie Willetts

Wm Jackson (Langley Green) Ltd

No book about Langley and district would be complete without a mention of local builders Wm Jackson of Langley Green; they were synonymous with all that went on for almost 100 years. They were established towards the end of the last century, 1897 I believe, and carried on until 1995 when they went into liquidation.

Wherever people went they would say "You can always tell Jackson's work by the quality of the brickwork".

They were involved in work for most of the local firms, and especially for the Local Education Authority - building the County High School (Oldbury Grammar School, now Langley High) in 1926; Bristnall Hall School in 1928/29; Moat Farm Junior in 1938: Warley High, Pound Road and Perryfields Senior 1953/54; and memorably Langley Carnegie Library in 1908.

Fred Broadbent

Langley Village Clock Tower Project

A comprehensive renewal and enhancement programme has been undertaken in Langley Village, improving the shops, pavements and car parks and installing CCTV.

It has been funded by the Black Country Development Corporation and co-ordinated by the BCDC and Sandwell Council in association with the Langley Traders.

These three organisations decided on a clock tower feature to be included in the area, with a sundial on one side, the three remaining faces to be designed by local school children.

From an educational view point this scheme has provided a unique opportunity for the children to gain new skills while working on curriculum subjects, such as local history, land use and environmental issues, with the added bonus of a remarkable piece of public art as a permanent reminder of their efforts.

from Council press release

The children involved in the project from Langley Primary School at the official handing-over ceremony on 16th October 1997.

In June 1997 fifty-four year five children were set the task of designing and making three decorative panels for the sundial, representing their thoughts on the past, present and future of Langley.

The children were divided into groups to create designs, which they sketched first and then reproduced on computer, with the help of staff from Sandwell's Education Micro-technology Unit.

The next task was to produce designs on large panels with the help of Nick Cole, an art student on placement with them. The final panels were chosen and were then manufactured by J B Joyce, Clockmakers of Whitchurch.

The children were really excited at the prospect of going on coaches to the Training Development Centre in Pope's Lane to produce the work. Finding out more about Langley in the past and questioning grandparents and neighbours brought the project more to life and further increased their enthusiasm.

Once the sundial was actually in place by the "Crosswells" Inn, the children started to appreciate the importance of their work and that it was something to be proud of and to show future generations

As a direct result of the success of this project, Langley Primary School and J B Joyce were presented with a "Quality in Partnership" award by the Mayor at the Sandwell Council House, Oldbury.

Ann Whitlock, Deputy Headteacher Langley Primary School

The future of the area lies with this generation . . .

Select Bibliography

"A Short History of Chance and Hunt"

Beaver, Rev Christopher M - "St Michael & All Angels'
  Langley a parish profile"

"Borough of Oldbury Official Souvenir to commemorate the
  Coronation of HM Queen Elizabeth II 2/6/53"

"Borough of Oldbury Royal Charter of Incorporation 1935"

"Borough of Oldbury Souvenir Programme Opening of
  Langley Baths 8/5/37"

Caddick, James H & Hildred, Trevor - "The Red Bricks by the
  Pool"

Dingley, Cyril S - "The Story of BIP"

Hackwood, Frederick William - "Oldbury & Round About"

"Langley & Langley Green Recalled"

"Made In Oldbury Souvenir Handbook"

McKean, Rev Henry - "Picturesque Oldbury"

Pearce, A A L - "Oldbury Grammar School 1904 - 1974. A
  short history"

Threlfall, R E - "The Story of 100 Years of Phosphorous Making "

Tranter, Judith - "Down Memory Lane: reminiscences of a
  Langley Green Couple"

Wakeman, H - "A Venture in Faith". A short history of Warley
  Institutional Church, 1906 -1956

"Zion, Langley Green. The First 200 Years 1790 - 1990"

Copies of other brochures and maps of the area are available for consultation at Langley Library, Barrs Street, Oldbury, West Midlands B68 8QT (tel: 0121 552 1680). We are always interested in copying old brochures, leaflets and magazines of local interest.

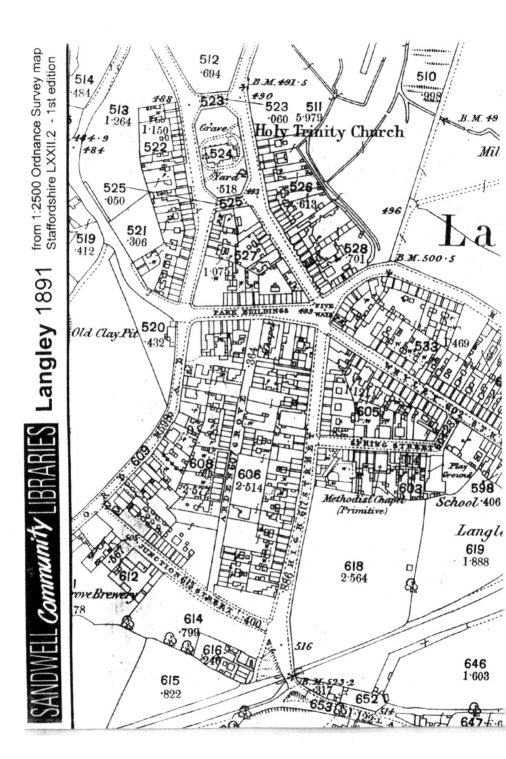

512
·694

514
·484

510

·998

B.M. 491·5

490

B.M. 49

513
1·264

488

523

523
·060

511
5·979

Holy Trinity Church

Mil

464·9
484

522

1·150

Grave

524

525

525
·050

Yard
·518

493

521
·306

526

·613

496

519
·412

527
1·075

528
·701

B.M. 500·5

La

Old Clay Pit

520
·432

PARK BUILDINGS

FIVE WAYS

533
469

Chapel

364

609

608

606
2·514

605

598

WEY ...

SPRING STREET

602

Play Ground

603

Methodist Chapel
(Primitive)

School ·406

505

Junction Street

612

Brewery

614
·799

618
2·564

Langl

619
1·888

615
·822

616

646
1·603

B.M. 523·2

652

653

647

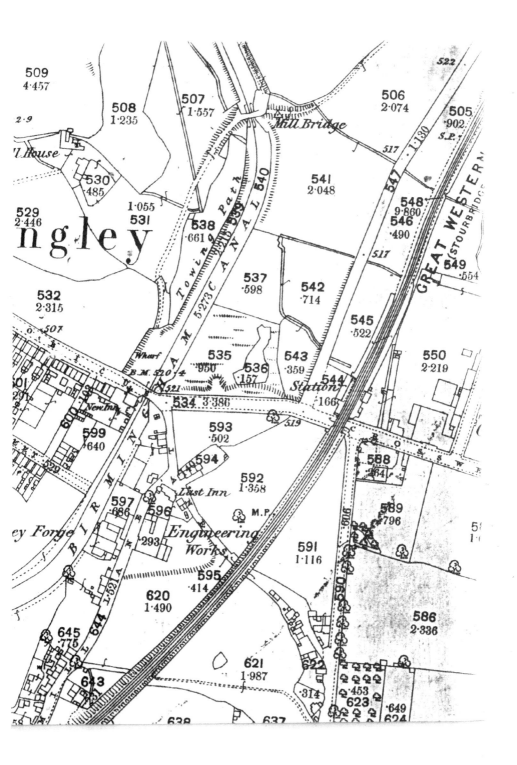

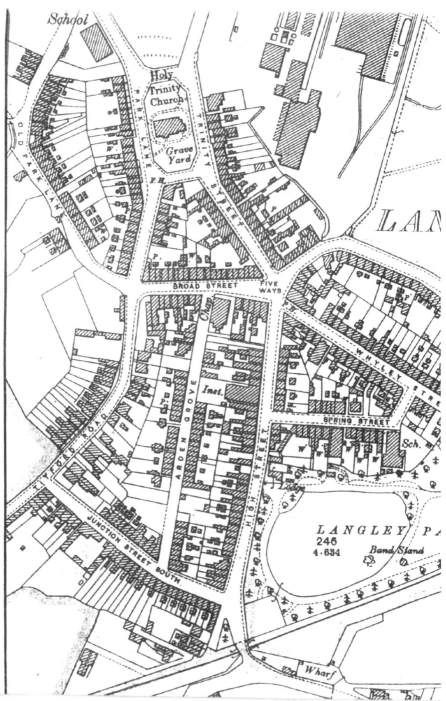

Langley 1904

from 1:2500 Ordnance Survey map
Staffordshire LXXII.2 - 2nd edition

School

Holy
Trinity
Church

Grave
Yard

OLD PARK LANE

PARK LANE

W.

P.H.

TRINITY STREET

P.

P.

P.

W.

BROAD STREET

FIVE
WAYS

LAN

LANGLEY PA

ARDEN GROVE

Inst.

Char

WHYLEY STRE

SPRING STREET

Sch.

TITFORD ROAD

HIGH STREET

W.

W.

W.

W.

W.

Lodge

246
4·634

Band Stand

JUNCTION STREET SOUTH

Wharf

Band

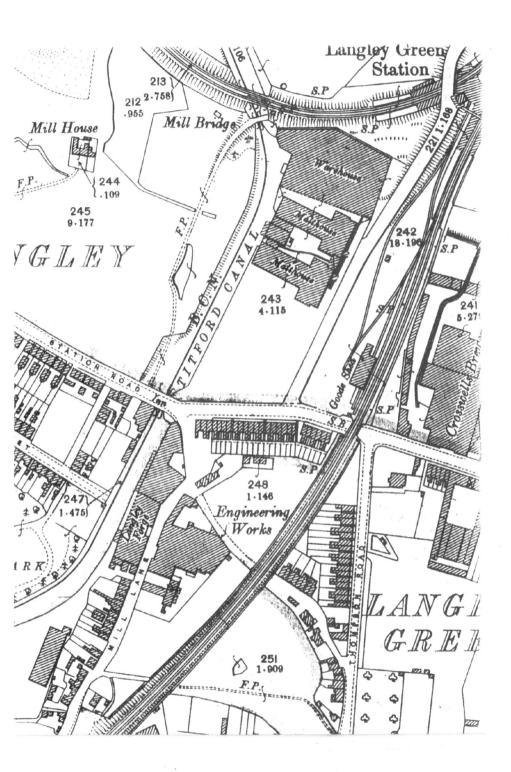

Langley 1919

from 1:2500 Ordnance Survey map
Staffordshire LXXII.2 - 3rd edition

SANDWELL Community LIBRARIES

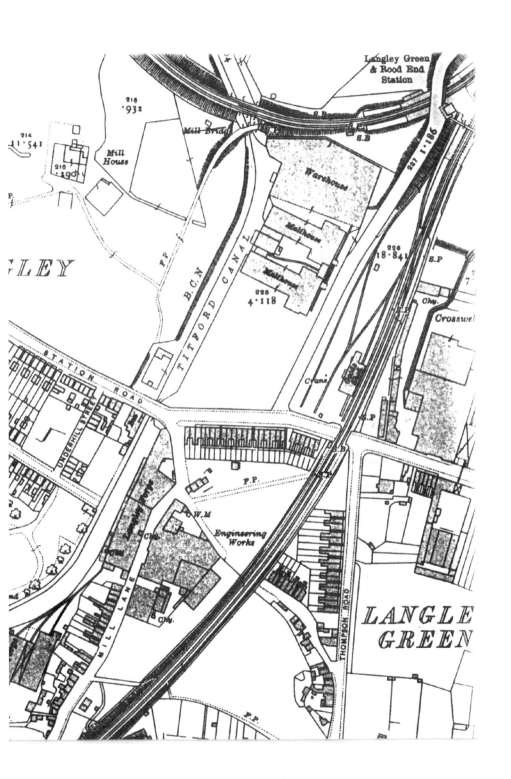

Langley 1938

from 1:2500 Ordnance Survey map
Staffordshire LXXII.2 – 4th edition

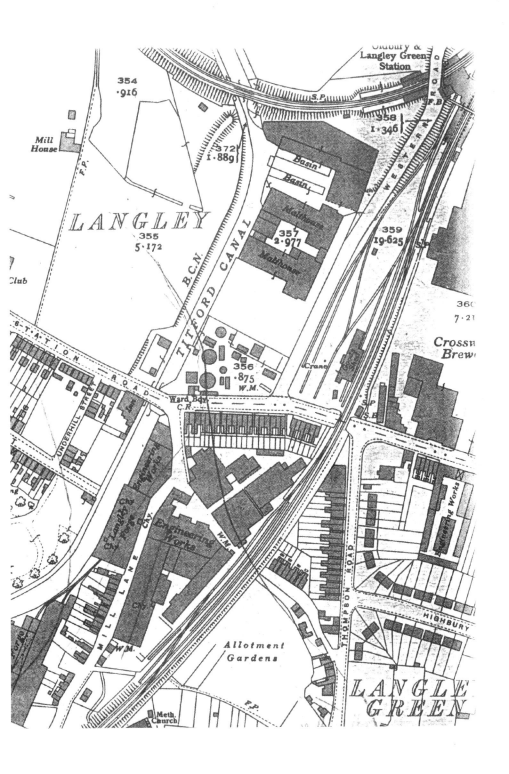

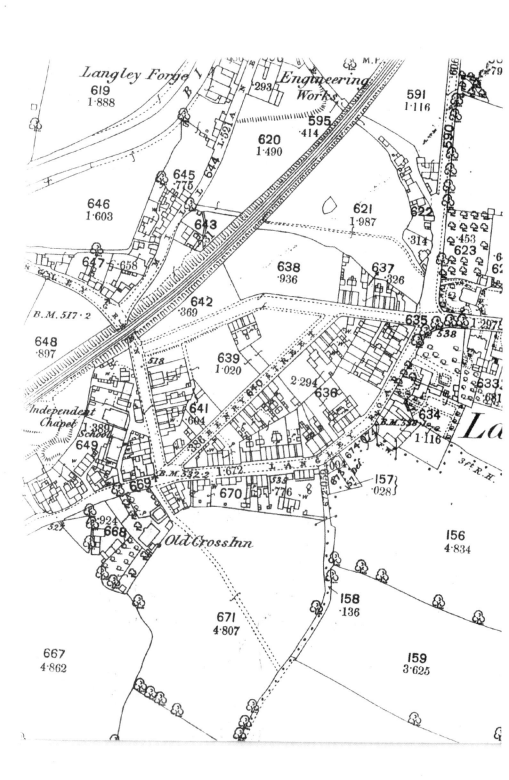

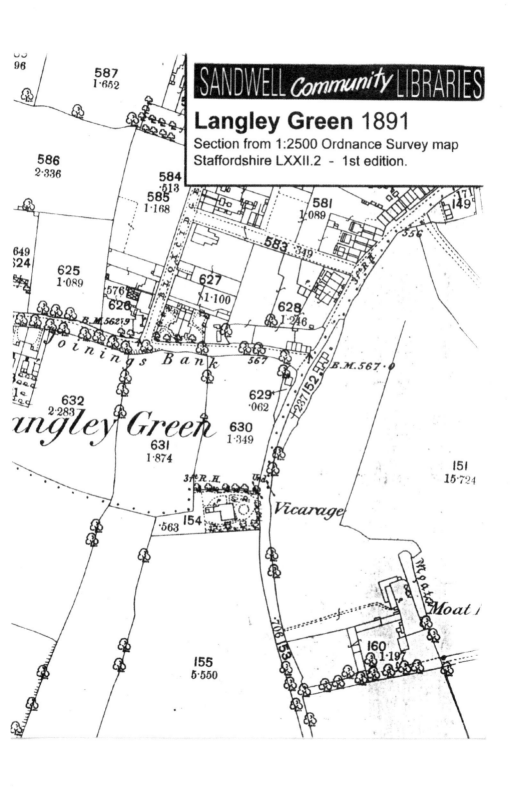

SANDWELL *Community* **LIBRARIES**

Langley Green 1891
Section from 1:2500 Ordnance Survey map
Staffordshire LXXII.2 - 1st edition.

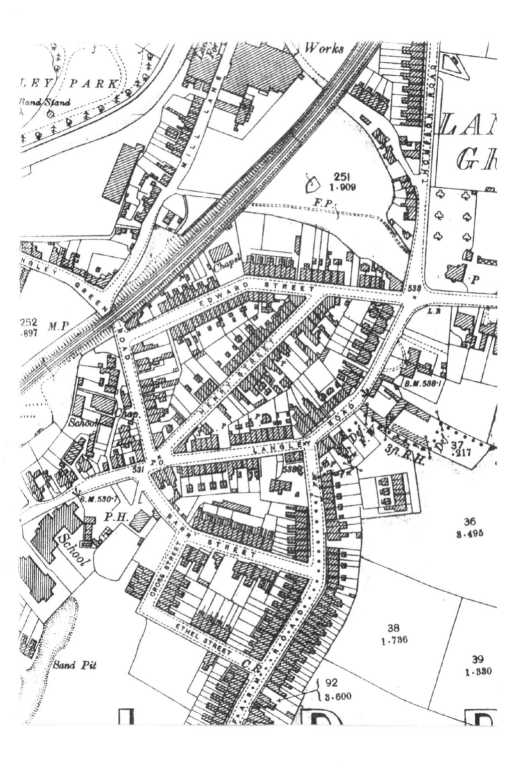

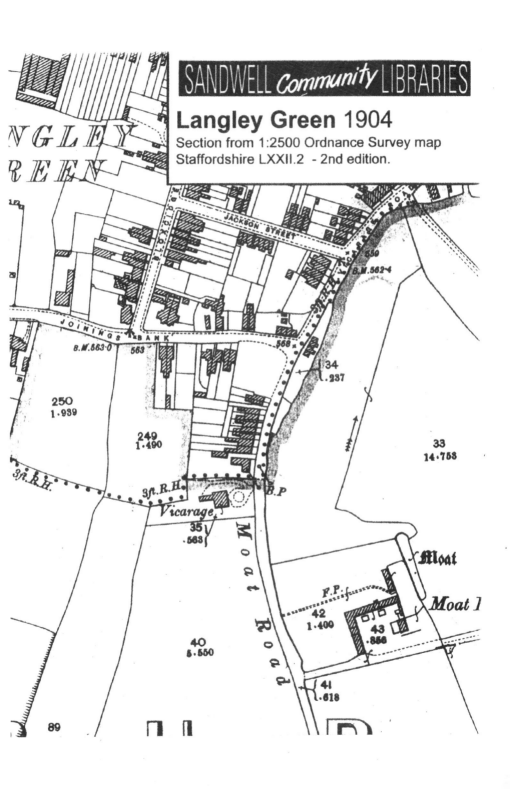

SANDWELL *Community* LIBRARIES

Langley Green 1904
Section from 1:2500 Ordnance Survey map
Staffordshire LXXII.2 - 2nd edition.

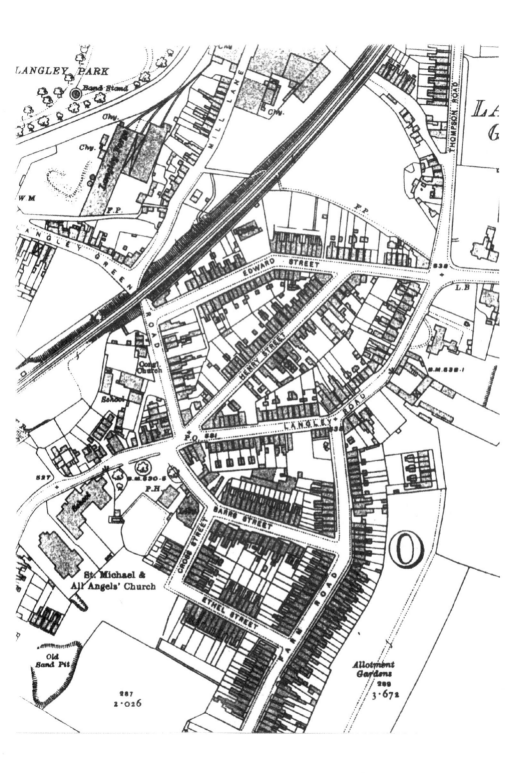

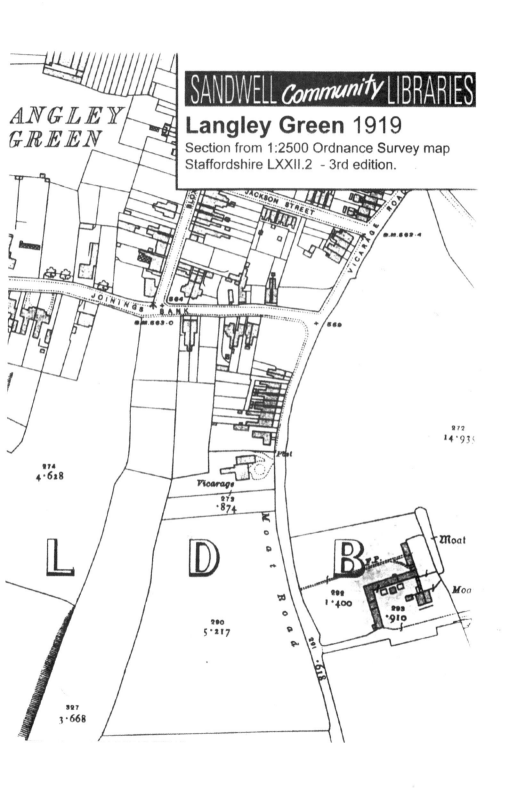

ANGLEY
GREEN

SANDWELL *Community* LIBRARIES
Langley Green 1919
Section from 1:2500 Ordnance Survey map
Staffordshire LXXII.2 - 3rd edition.

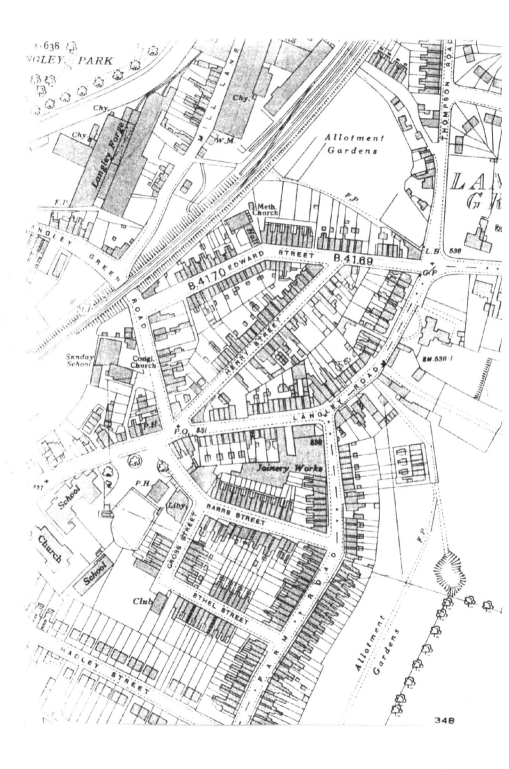

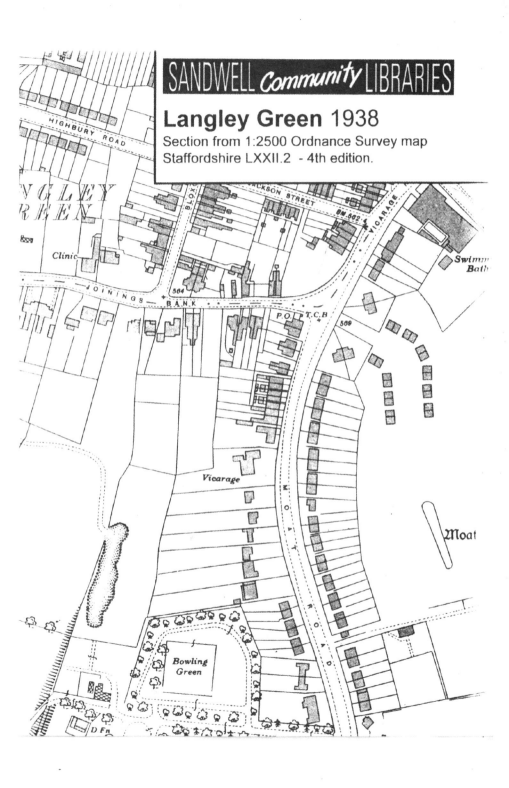

SANDWELL *Community* LIBRARIES

Langley Green 1938
Section from 1:2500 Ordnance Survey map
Staffordshire LXXII.2 - 4th edition.

Index

Photographs and maps are indicated thus: *204*